PAINTING
WITH WOOL

# PAINTING

## WITH WOOL

16 Artful Projects to
NEEDLE FELT

DANI IVES

In 2015, I quit what I thought would be my lifetime career and began my pursuit to become a full-time maker and artist. That decision didn't come quickly or easily, but I certainly don't regret it. Being able to put my creative skills to use daily has been an incredible reward for the amount of work and practice I put forth in the beginning and every day since.

I never could have predicted this path, which has been both awesome and terrifying. I grew up wanting to work with animals, and that's what I did as a conservation educator in a zoo setting. Over nearly ten years I helped educate thousands of students and adults about animals, their habitats, and the things we can do to be responsible stewards of wildlife and of our planet.

But one day, I had a seemingly innocent conversation about crafts with a coworker that would later have a profound impact on my future. She introduced me to needle felting and explained that you could make cute animal figurines with the process. I ordered some supplies from Etsy, and I was hooked. Needle felting became a way for me to unwind, relax, and work with my hands at the end of the day. (If you're new to felting, you'll soon discover how meditative it can be!) I started creating a menagerie of animal figurines, and then I jumped into the world of selling on Etsy and at local craft shows. My wool creations branched out into potted plants, pin cushions, and jewelry. Then, a couple of years into my felting journey, I tried my hand at a two-dimensional wool picture. It was a revelation! I realized that this style was perfect for me, because it was not only more artistically fulfilling, but it was also a challenge. I soon discovered that there weren't any resources to guide me down this path. But I knew what I wanted to accomplish, so I kept experimenting and testing ideas. Finally, I've arrived at a place in my work that is special and worth sharing with others. Working with fibers in a manner that mimics the look and feel of traditional painting has been a result of investing thousands of hours in my practice.

Whether or not you're new to needle felting, my goal for this book is to give you a peek at the potential that wool can offer as an artful medium. The scope of possibilities is truly endless. As I continue my felting practice, I'm learning every day. In these pages, I offer you the methods and techniques that have helped me the most as I've grown into my medium. Together, we'll work on technical skills as well as creative skills. I truly believe that everyone can be creative.

Every person who wants to be an artist can be an artist. But your creativity is a muscle that needs to be worked and tested regularly. Nurture your creative skills and help them grow by testing out new ideas and challenging old assumptions. When I picked up a felting needle for the first, second, and even hundredth time, I wasn't sure that what I set out to make at that moment was possible, but all I had to do was try. Every piece is an opportunity to learn and grow.

If you're ever hesitant about trying something new, consider that stepping out of your comfort zone can be a fast track to opening the floodgates to your creativity. It helps you look at subjects, techniques, and results with fresh eyes. It's so important to do this every now and then, especially if you're finding yourself yearning for a change. In the beginning, you might not get the results you want, and that's okay. Expect to fall short at first. I surely expect to when I'm trying something new. But I know that if I keep working and keep practicing, my efforts will pay off.

The projects in this book offer a range of ways to practice using wool as a medium for surface design. If you've never delved into the world of fiber arts (welcome!), you'll be surprised at how fulfilling it is to work with something so textural. Holding and manipulating the fibers and knowing that each of them passed through your hands is a unique feeling, and I've witnessed many students experience this.

I've been teaching needle felting techniques since 2015. Taking on the role of educator was second nature once I was comfortable with my skills. I teach in-person workshops, master classes, and lead online courses all about needle felting. I've studied what is most helpful for students to understand and learn, and I truly enjoy watching others discover the magic of painting with wool. I hope you enjoy creating the projects in this book as much as I have. After you've practiced and experimented with these projects, you'll be looking everywhere for things to embellish with needle felting. I hope you take the lessons and steps I've presented and use them as a springboard for creating all kinds of artful projects. Now, grab your needle and wool, and let's get started!

Chapter

# 1

# THE BASICS

# Why Needle Felting

Once you learn a few basic techniques, the process of needle felting is very easy. You're literally just poking fibers to make them stick together. What's happening is the barbed needle is grabbing wool fibers and tangling them with the base fabric and other surrounding fibers. Each wool fiber is textured on a microscopic level, so creating friction among the fibers with your needle links them together, creating felt. But it's the artistic practice you will use to create something artful. Learning how to "see" your subject in a way that you can transfer to your medium is key. The learning curve for creating art isn't always in the materials, it's in the development of how you see your subject. My goal for these projects is to minimize the initial learning curve and to help you build basic felting skills that will allow you to portray your own subjects later.

I often hear from students that they are intimidated by needle felting. But once they learn the different steps that simplify processes like blending colors, adding highlights, and laying down shadows for dimension and shape, they feel like creating artful pieces is not only achievable but fun! I also hear (and wholeheartedly agree) that needle felting is addictive. It's easy to get lost in a piece, to keep working and going until your art is complete. Needle felting offers instant gratification. When you poke a fiber into place, that's where it exists, regardless of what happens around it. You can layer on top of that fiber or lay more right beside it. You can push it and pull it with the needle to alter its line. But my favorite quality about wool as a medium is that it's extremely forgiving. Unlike ink or paint, if you lay down some fibers and decide that you don't like that color or placement, up to a certain point, you can simply lift the fibers back up with no harm to the fabric below. Making changes or reworking your art has never been easier—once you pass the "point of no return," you can still revise your work by simply adding fiber on top! Experimenting with fibers and testing the possibilities with felting needles is half the fun and will help you develop your own favorite techniques.

# Getting Started

For every project, you'll need a few basic supplies. Felting needles, wool, a base fabric on to which you'll add your design (for two-dimensional projects), and a felting work surface for your tabletop or lap. There are many options for each of these supplies, and you'll want to experiment to see what works best for you. For the tutorials in later chapters, I share the supplies I used for each project.

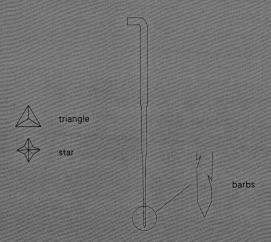

triangle

star

barbs

## FELTING NEEDLES

Felting needles have one-way barbs that help you do all the felting magic. When you poke the needle through the wool and into the base fabric, those barbs are grabbing wool fibers and taking them into the base fabric and the foam pad beneath (see above). That's where they stay when you lift your needle back out. The same thing happens if you're creating a three-dimensional piece and poking the wool into itself. The fibers become tangled and intertwined, and this is the process of creating felt.

Needles come in many variations. There are different sizes—the higher the size number, the smaller the gauge, or diameter, of the needle, and vice versa. Smaller needles are typically used more for surface detail and finishing work, since they don't leave behind noticeable holes, and you can manipulate small amounts of fiber more easily. They're also better to use when felting with fine fibers like merino. Larger needles are great for grabbing more fibers, which makes the work a bit quicker, especially for three-dimensional work.

Felting needles are also available with differently shaped tips or blades, which correspond to the number of edges the needle tip has or the way the needle tip is created. A triangle needle has three sides, which means it has three edges that have barbs. A star needle has four edges with barbs. The more barbs, the more fibers your needle can grab at once, helping you felt more quickly. A spiral needle has a twist to the blade, giving it added strength. There are even specialty felting needles that offer different combinations and orientations of barbs—you can also find needles that have just one or two barbs only on one edge for very specific placement of just a few fibers.

I prefer to use size 38 star felting needles for most projects. They tend to be stronger, and I like that the barbs are a little closer to the tip of the needle, allowing me to do shallow detail work.

I'm often asked when to replace felting needles, and truthfully, I just use my needles until I accidently bend or break them. The surface that I'm felting into is never that tightly woven or felted that it makes much of a difference whether the needle is brand-new or slightly dulled. Felting needles were originally created for large-scale felt-making for use in automobile, carpet, and musical instrument production, so they are quite industrious and tend to last a long time. That said, I do notice a needle if it is very dull, and I will replace it. If at some point during a project you feel like you're fighting the fibers or background fabric and more effort than normal is required to push through, check and see if a fresh needle might be the answer.

## MULTI-NEEDLE TOOLS

These allow you to easily hold anywhere from two to twenty needles at once and come in different sizes and arrangements to suit your needs. Multi-needle tools can help you cover more surface area quickly and can be very useful if you need to lay down a base layer before adding detail. You can skip these tools altogether and hold two needles next to each other as an alternative. This is my preferred method most of the time, but a six-needle tool is my go-to for laying down a single color at a large scale.

## WORK SURFACE

So far, I've found that the best work surface for my style of two-dimensional felting is a dense foam pad, often labeled *needle felting foam* by suppliers. The foam should be stiff but not hard or crumbly. This type of surface will allow you to create intense details and work a few layers of wool in one spot before it begins to break down. When the foam starts to break down, it will become indented and much softer. I prefer to use the foam when it's firm for detailed projects, so I move around the foam pad (front and back) with each new project. After it's been broken in with projects created over the entirety of its surface, I'll reuse the foam pad for pieces that don't require as much detail or felting. These pads come in a variety of sizes, and I try to use pieces that accommodate my entire design. However, if necessary, it's fine to felt a section and then move the foam pad to fit underneath the remaining area to be felted.

## FABRICS

There are so many possibilities available as a base fabric for your projects. My go-to choices are pure wool felt (1 mm thick) and linen. I've also had great success felting on cotton, cotton blends, velvet, and even burlap. Don't judge a fabric by its looks. My advice is to experiment and see what works and what you like best. Each fabric has its own feel and ability to accept the wool fibers. Test how well you can push a felting needle through; make sure the fabric isn't so dense that it causes the needle to bend or break. Consider staying away from fabrics with a lot of elasticity to avoid buckling and puckering. Before starting each project, I recommend preparing the fabric by getting out wrinkles as best you can.

## FIBERS

Different kinds of fibers will give you vastly different results when needle felting. In this book, I'll be using sheep's wool for the projects. But there are many different animal (and some plant) fibers that are possible to needle felt with. It's best to experiment to see what you like to work with and also how you prefer your finished projects to look. For beginners, it makes sense to start with what I consider the easiest preparation of wool: carded batts. These batts consist of shorter fibers that have been carded into a thick sheet called batting. This preparation allows you to use small chunks of wool at a time, blend colors easily, and create cleaner details with only a few fibers.

Other preparations can also be used with great results. Typically, I don't use much roving in my art, because it's more difficult to work into a piece in a neat way. Because roving is made of longer fibers that are combed in one direction, it's harder to break off small pieces, and the felting results can be very "hairy" and lumpy. However, it's possible to cut the fibers into smaller pieces of equal length and make a mini batt with your fingers. Use the color-mixing method on page 24 with the shorter roving fibers to make a texture that is easier to "paint" with.

## INTRODUCTION TO THE NEEDLE FELTING TECHNIQUE

There are different ways to create the same results when using a felting needle. I'm going to share what works for me as well as what I've noticed works well for my students. Once you're comfortable handling a felting needle, do what's easiest and safest for you.

### How to Hold the Felting Needle

I hold my needle with my thumb and first finger at the top near the lip and then rest the shaft of the needle on my middle and ring fingers. For me, this gives the most control of the needle and leads to fewer broken or bent needles. Another option is to hold the needle as you would a pencil. With this grasp, however, I've noticed that needles more easily break because of the extended range of the needle arc as the needle comes down to the felting surface—basically, the needle can bend when it's inserted into the fibers.

## The Felting Motion

To begin needle felting, poke the needle in and out of the wool fibers that you have placed on the background fabric. Most of the felting movement will come from the wrist and the forearm. Most importantly, make sure the needle is entering and exiting the felting surface in a straight in-and-out motion. This movement does not have to be vertical—a felting needle can be used at any angle, as long as its path is straight. Avoid movements of the hand or wrist that cause the needle to bend while inside the foam pad. Felting needles will bend and break with enough sideways stress and pressure. Bent needles are not safe to use, and it's best to discard them.

When poking, my needle inserts around half an inch, on average, into the felting surface and foam pad. This is when I'm covering a larger area with wool without much regard to fine details. Detail work tends to be much shallower. When concentrating on surface details, it's usually important for the fibers to remain mostly on top of the other fibers, and the deeper the needle is inserted, the more those fibers will be buried.

## Try It Out: Filling In a Shape

Grab a small piece of sheet felt and place it on the foam pad. Take an amount of wool smaller than your desired shape and place it inside the shape next to the outline. Begin felting the fibers along the outline to create the edge, then felt down the remaining fibers inside the shape. Grab another small amount of wool to continue filling in the shape. It's best to overlap the fibers a little each time you add more, which avoids creating unwanted seams or separations between each chunk of wool added. Continue until the shape is filled.

My favorite thing to demonstrate to new students is the forgiving nature of needle felting. If you mess up or change your mind on a color or texture, you can simply lift those fibers back up. Try it with the shape you just felted. Lift the sheet felt from the foam pad and notice the fuzzy back side; those fibers are the ones you pushed through with the felting needle. To remove the felted design, grab the edge of the wool shape and peel it off the sheet felt. Keep in mind that removing large sections of wool won't be easily done if you've already felted it tightly. If the fibers are flat and firm against the background fabric, and you have to really tug to get them loose, you could warp the background fabric by pulling too hard. At this point, it's best to layer more fibers on top to make the desired change, or start over.

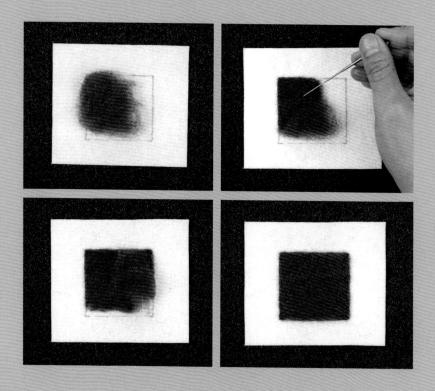

## HOW MUCH WOOL DO YOU NEED?

To roughly determine how much wool you'll need to complete a project, you can break off pieces of the batts and lay them on top of the pattern to eyeball the amount required to cover that surface. Keep in mind you'll be condensing the fibers as you felt them, so I always err on the side of having too much wool at the ready rather than too little.

# 2

# TRIED & TRUE TECHNIQUES

These techniques are my go-to methods when creating wool paintings. The projects in this book will occasionally refer to these, plus learning them will be a valuable asset to add to your skills bank.

# HOW TO CUSTOM-MIX WOOL COLORS

Learning how to create intermediate blends of two or more wool colors can be invaluable when trying to find the perfect shade for a project. This blending technique is easiest to do with shorter wool fibers. Take a small amount of each of the shades you'd like to blend. Stack one on the other and grab each end with your hands, ensuring you have some of every color in each hand, and split the stack by pulling it apart. Repeat the stack/pull/split process until the fibers are uniformly mixed. Using this method, you can create a completely customized wool palette by making different combinations of solid colors and even mixing newly blended fibers with each other.

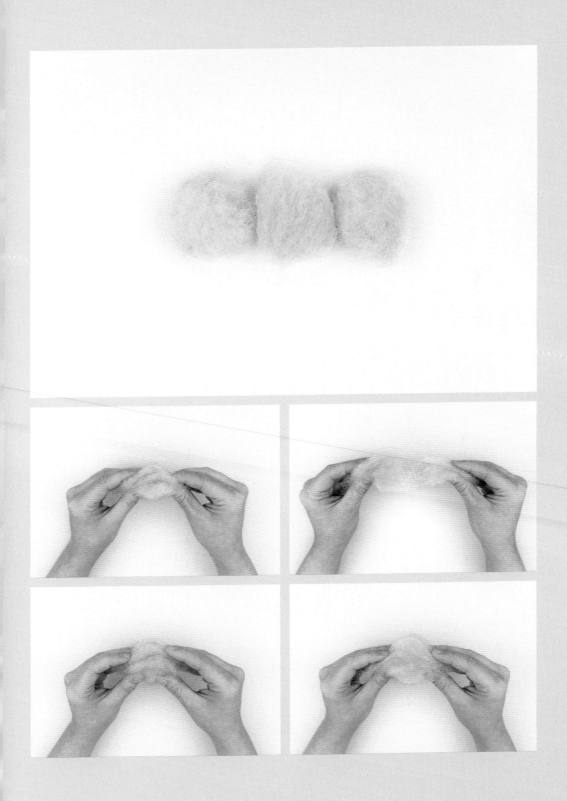

# HOW TO CREATE SEAMLESS COLOR BLENDS

The trick to creating colors that blend seamlessly one into the next is gentle layering and application. When blending from one color to the next shade, there will be quite a bit of overlapping. But the overlapping layers need to be "transparent." The fibers themselves are obviously not transparent, but the layer of fibers needs to be thin enough to allow the color below to show through. This can be done with thinner and thinner layers to increase the blend area. Use the tips of the felting needles to scrape at and feather the top fiber layer to disperse them as needed. An important thing to keep in mind when creating these gentle blends is that the layers added to the top need to stay on top rather than being pushed deeply down into the piece. Use shallow pokes of the felting needle to accomplish this, and consider using needles that have barbs closer to the tip (like my favorite, the size 38 star).

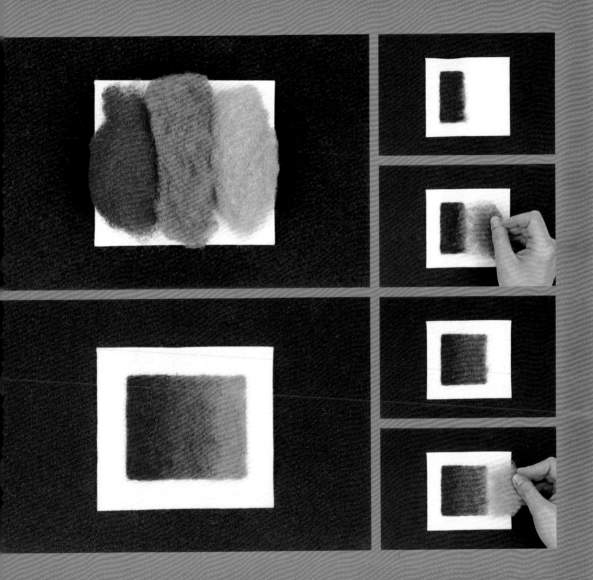

# HOW TO CREATE THIN LINES

Learning how to create thin lines of any length can really enhance the level of detail you can achieve in your wool art. You'll be limited a little by the type of wool you're using, so I recommend practicing on a scrap piece of felt or fabric to see what is possible. First, manipulate the wool fibers into a long, thin strand. This can be done by gently tugging at the fibers down the length to separate and thin them out. Next, gently roll the fibers together to make a long rope. If it's too thick, try tugging the fibers to thin them out a little more. If it's too thin, add more fibers. When the rope of wool is the right thickness, anchor one end of the fibers into the background fabric. Using your spare hand, gently keep the fibers taut and guide them into place with the needle. A very light and shallow touch with the needle is necessary to not disturb the fibers and make them buckle, as well as to keep the thin line visible. Sometimes it's helpful to avoid poking into the center of the line. Instead, poke the edge of the line only if possible. It's like you're poking the wool just enough to get it into place, and then letting it sit there undisturbed. Be sure to anchor the other end of the line.

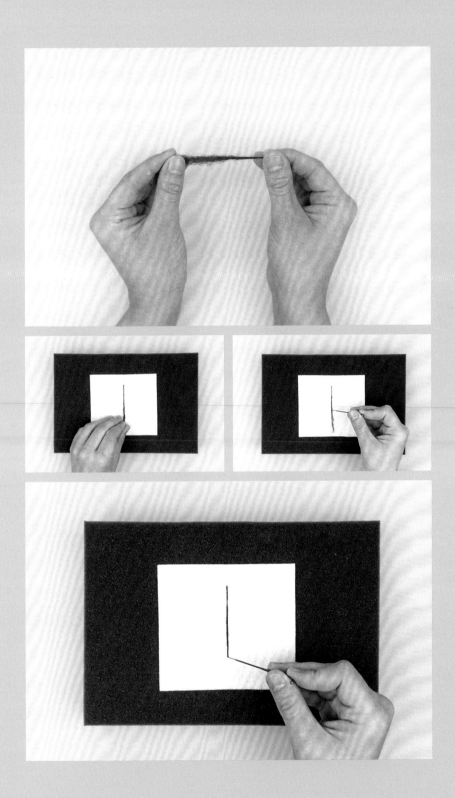

# HOW TO CREATE SHARP EDGES

When a bold line or a crisp edge is important to a design, my favorite trick to use is a technique I like to call "poke and drag." Using one needle, poke the tip right along the edge of the wool that should be a sharp line. Without losing contact with the surface of the wool or fabric, gently lift the needle and drag it along the edge of the wool for a short distance, then poke the dragged fibers down. Continue poking and dragging the needle along the edge to tuck in stray fibers and create a crisp line. For this technique to be most effective, there needs to be plenty of wool available for the needle to grab. If only a few fibers need to be tucked in, poke at them with the needle at a 45- or 30-degree angle to the work surface until they disappear.

# USING COLOR IN EFFECTIVE WAYS

1. Consider some of the colors I used within this dog portrait. Reflections of the outdoor light and blue sky can be seen in her eyes, nose, and bottom lip. You'll even see a bit of purple mixed with the blue to create more dimension and interest. The yellow ball in her mouth is a combination of six shades, ranging from light cream for the highlight to deep orange for the shadow. Her fur, at quick glance in real life or in the reference photo, is basically one color: gold. (Similarly, that's typically how we think of a person's hair: we call it just brown or black, etc.) But in the felted piece, I used many shades of brown to create the layers and depth that exist. The darker browns are reserved for shadows and inner layers of fur. The lighter brown and creams are used for outer layers, highlights, and shiny pieces.

2. Playing with color for reflective surfaces is a great exercise and can yield surprising results. The colors that make the shape and dimension of this red apple include variations of red, orange, pink, yellow, green, blue, and deep purple. The darker shades of purple and red are used to push that part of the apple surface backward. The lighter tints bring those sections of apple forward and upward. The concentration of lighter colors in the reflection spot help to show that the surface of the apple is smooth and shiny.

3. The shape of the color variations you add to a piece can make a big difference, too. A hummingbird is covered in tiny, reflective feathers. To illustrate that, in a few sections I first added a darker base color, then layered small dots of lighter shades on top of the base color to give the impression of individual feathers. Through the addition of these small dots rather than just a layer of color, individual feathers take shape and give the bird a beautiful texture. This is most noticeable on the hummingbird's ruby neck and green head.

# TRANSFERRING AN IMAGE OR A PATTERN

A few transferring techniques can be borrowed from other crafts like embroidery. If your felting fabric is thin enough, a lightbox or window can be used to trace a bold image outline. An iron-on transfer pen is also an option, as well as a pen with air-dissolvable ink. For me, the quickest way to transfer an image is to size a photo or to draw an image to the exact scale needed and transfer the lines by poking through the paper to the fabric and connecting the dots with a pen.

Here's an example:

1. Place your pattern exactly where it is to be transferred onto to the fabric. Center the pattern and fabric over the felting foam. Pin the image so that it will not move. Use two or three sewing pins or a couple of felting needles to secure the pattern.

2. Using a felting needle, begin poking the outlines (and other notable lines or shading demarcations). Press the needle down to where the shaft is wider to make a hole large enough to easily see. This is especially important when using a fabric with a weave (like linen).

3. Make only a few pokes at a time, then lift the image and connect the holes with a pen. Only working with a few dots at a time and comparing the needle marks with the image will help avoid confusion and mixing up outlines. Plus, depending on the fabric, poked holes can disappear easily if the fabric is moved too much.

4. Continue this method until the entire image is transferred onto the fabric.

## Keep in mind

It's important not to remove the pattern or image until all the desired outlines have been transferred. Removing the pattern will make it hard to line up again later.

If you're having trouble seeing the needle holes, poking your pen through the paper to directly mark the fabric is another option. This method is less precise but can be helpful with thicker fabrics. For darker fabrics, try using a white or light-colored gel pen.

When felting over a transferred pattern, be sure to cover the ink lines with wool fibers. As layers are added and more felting occurs inside the lines, the fibers will naturally be pulled toward the area most felted, which is often away from the outlines. Directly covering the outlines or extending the colors beyond them a tiny amount will prevent any pen marks from showing in the end.

## Dealing with Needle Marks

Sometimes felting needles can leave behind small marks or holes. There are a few things to try to make these disappear. Adding thin layers of wool with shallow pokes will help to cover existing holes without creating noticeable new ones. Typically, the denser the wool layers on a piece (not necessarily thicker, but the tighter the felted wool is), the less likely the holes will be a problem. Carefully brushing over the needle marks with the tip of a felting needle, or even a finger, will help to disguise them. Lastly, switching to a smaller gauge needle, like a 40 or 42, will help to create a softer, smoother top layer.

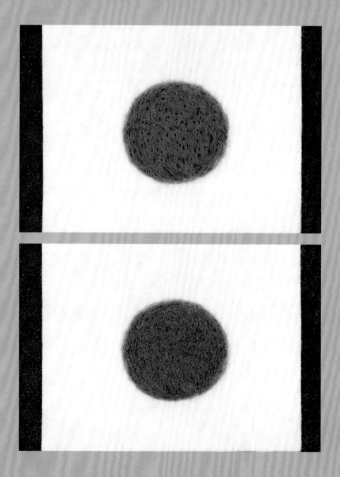

## Removing Work from the Foam Pad

As you're felting, the fibers that the needle is pushing through the fabric are also inserted into the foam pad. When your wool painting is finished, you must lift the piece up, thus pulling those fibers out of the foam. This can seem daunting at first, but rest assured that I've never had a piece be damaged by this process. The trick is to lift slowly and evenly, being careful not to tug too much from one spot. Keep your hand close to the foam pad, rather than pulling on a distant fabric edge.

      The back side will be quite fuzzy, and you'll notice all the places where the needle poked through. Usually, it's much fuzzier where details are concentrated. You can keep the back side as is, or iron down fibers to flatten them. (I often use steam to make quick work of this. Since there is little agitation with using an iron, this small amount of steam won't cause the fibers to shrink or felt any more.) Keep in mind that any time you iron a wool painting (from the back or front), it will likely alter the fibers on the front of the design at least a little. You can always give it a few needle nudges to move anything back into place if necessary.

# CARING FOR WOOL PAINTINGS

There are many options for displaying wool art and caring for felted pieces. The question I'm asked most often is "How do you keep it from getting dusty?" You always have the option of putting a piece behind glass in a frame or shadowbox. Personally, I prefer not to use glass, because it can take away from the textural aspect of a piece, especially if the glass is touching it. If a displayed piece gets a little dusty, tap it from the back or consider blowing it off. A can of compressed air could help; just be sure to do it from a safe distance in order to not concentrate the airflow too much and move the fibers. You can help protect wool art from moths or other harmful insects by adding a drop or two of lavender essential oil to the back side of the frame or to a piece of the fabric that is wrapped around an embroidery hoop edge—don't apply the oil where it could potentially seep through to the front of your artwork. But unless you're storing a piece in a dark closet or attic, this likely won't be a problem.

Any felted item that is usable or wearable (clothing, table linens, etc.) should be carefully hand-washed to avoid potential damage to the design. If agitated too much, the wool fibers will continue to felt together and can warp the design or overall fabric. Use a detergent that is safe for wool and designed for hand-washables. If a felted part of an item is somehow damaged or stained, you can easily fix it by adding fibers and felting over the top of the trouble area. Easy peasy!

# DEVELOPING YOUR STYLE

As an artist or a maker, it's important to develop your own style. It's certainly okay to mimic the style of others as you're learning or exploring new directions, but if you're making work to call your own (or even sell), nailing down a style that is recognizable as unique to yourself is essential. Think of a few of your favorite artists or makers. Chances are you'd know their work if you saw it, even if it wasn't labeled, because they've created work with their own spin. It's also okay for your style to evolve. It's inevitable, because your skills will improve, or you might become a little bored with doing the same type of work over and over.

If you're unsure of your style, start taking note of things in your life that attract your attention. What are you drawn to? What type of art do you decorate your home with? What colors and patterns do you use to fill your wardrobe? These things will give you some clues as to what your style might involve. If you're an artist who enjoys drawing, painting, pastels, etc., are you more apt to produce pieces that are loose, flowy, and more abstract, or do you tend to squeeze in every detail as accurately as possible? I'm the latter. I have a penchant for realism, and I strive to portray subjects in wool as they appear in real life. But I greatly admire and try to emulate artists whose style is completely different from my own. You may not stick with a style you're testing, but occasionally trying something new can help bring dimension to your work or can help you develop a process or method to use down the road.

The greatest thing about art is you can create whatever you want. You'll create things you love and things you hate. Just keep creating. There are no rules, there are only techniques that you can modify to fit your needs. From this book, I want you to take away the techniques that are useful to you, modify them however you see fit, and then create a style that is uniquely YOU. Use the tools and practice you develop here to show the world your art.

# BEGINNER PROJECTS

The projects in this chapter are perfect for novice felters, but they're also great if you don't have a lot of time to commit. These projects offer ways to help you practice handling the needle and wool and become accustomed to the needle felting process, and will introduce you to basic painting with wool techniques, such as laying down larger areas of color, defining shapes, and getting sharp, distinct lines.

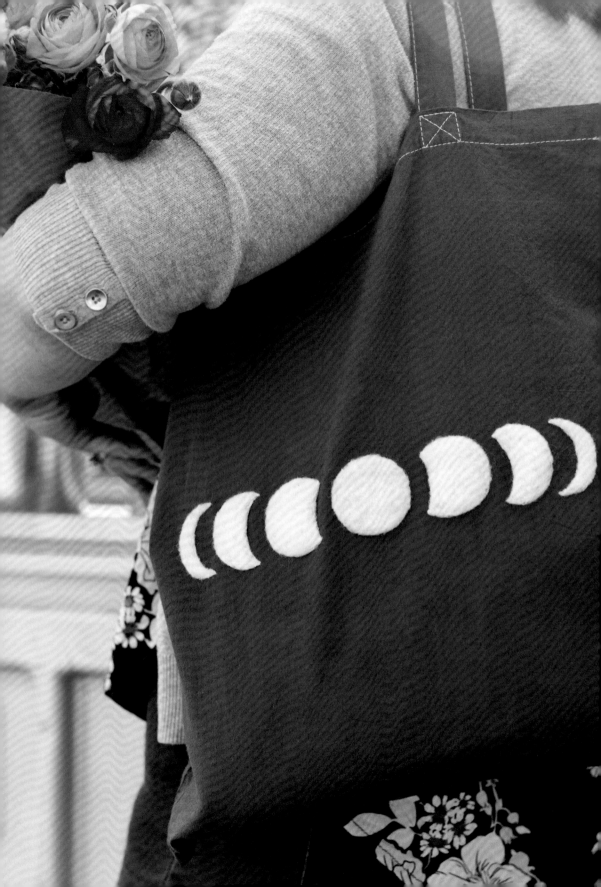

# Moon Phase Tote Bag

This is the perfect project for dipping your toes into painting with wool. The design is simple and quick to complete, but it offers good practice for creating sharp edges and manipulated shapes. And when you're finished, you can show it off wherever you go!

**Approximate Time to Complete: 1 hour**

## Supplies

Moon phase pattern (page 130)

Pen

Cotton tote bag*

Foam pad

Carded wool batt (shown in white)

Size 38 star felting needle

*The tote shown here is made of a very thin cotton fabric. It is possible to felt designs onto thicker cotton fabrics, but it will take more time and effort. In an inconspicuous location, test that the felting needle will travel easily through the fabric before getting started.

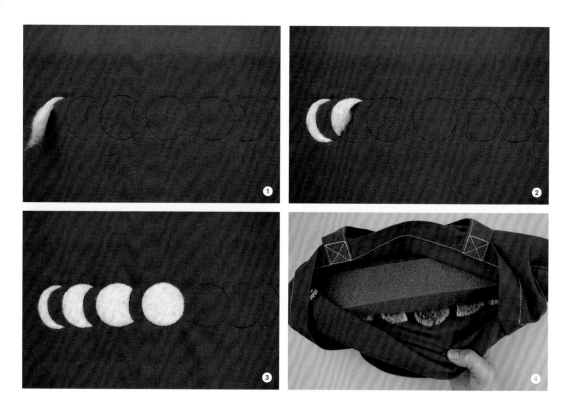

### Prep the pattern

Insert the foam pad between the two layers of the tote bag, center it under the pattern, and transfer using the method on page 34. If the foam pad isn't large enough to fit under the entire design, work it in parts, finishing as much of the design as possible before moving the foam pad to work on the rest.

### Create the moon phases

Beginning with a small amount of wool, start filling in the first moon by tacking the wool into the point of the crescent and following the curve of the outline. Attaching the wool along the corners and outline first is the easiest and quickest way to keep the shape true to the pattern without having to adjust the outlines later (photo ❶).

Continue filling in the moon phases until complete (photo ❷).

Fill in thin spots or level out any ridges or bumps by adding small amounts of wool. If needed, adjust the shape of a moon by poking the outline from the side at a 45-degree or smaller angle (photo ❸).

### Finish

Carefully lift the tote fabric from the foam pad (photo ❹).

Head to the farmers' market with your new tote!

---

Recommended·
Iron the felted moon phases from the back and/or front.

---

**Tip.** When moving from one part of a pattern to the next, choosing a piece in close proximity to what has already been felted will help keep any fabric buckling to a minimum. I typically move from left to right with simple designs. If the fabric or pattern seems to shift as you felt from one part to the next, just stick to the transferred pattern and everything should straighten out once the foam pad is removed. It's okay to lift the pattern from the foam pad while you're in the middle of a project; just keep in mind that the bulkiness of the wool on the back side might prevent it from laying completely flat again. (Ironing the fuzzy back side can help to flatten those fibers, if necessary.) For many projects this isn't a problem, but I avoid lifting very detailed pieces from the foam until finished.

Many beginners are often curious about how thick the wool of the final piece should be after it's felted. This is up to personal preference. Some felters like a bit of relief in their work, and others (like myself) prefer flatter pieces. Ideally, I like to keep my pieces as flat as possible while also making sure the wool is thick enough to not let any background fabric peek through. Keep in mind, it's much easier to add wool than take it away once you start felting. But if you find yourself with too much wool in one spot, you can remove it—carefully. With one hand, press down on the wool that has already been felted to keep it in place. With the other hand, gently pull at the loose fibers that you want to remove. Take away small tufts at a time until enough has been removed.

# Geometric Pillow

**Approximate Time to Complete: 2 to 3 hours**

## Supplies

Triangle pattern

Pen

18" × 18" (46 × 46 cm) blue linen pillowcase

4 colors of carded wool batts (shown in fuchsia, neon green, deep kelly green, bright blue)

Foam pad

Size 38 star felting needle

I've always found the triangle to be a fun shape for creating interesting compositions and patterns. For this pillow cover, I knew I wanted the design to be heavier in one corner, but other than that I had no plans for a pattern. To decide on my layout, I cut out multiple copies of the same triangle and started placing them on the pillow cover and moving them around until it looked pleasantly unbalanced.

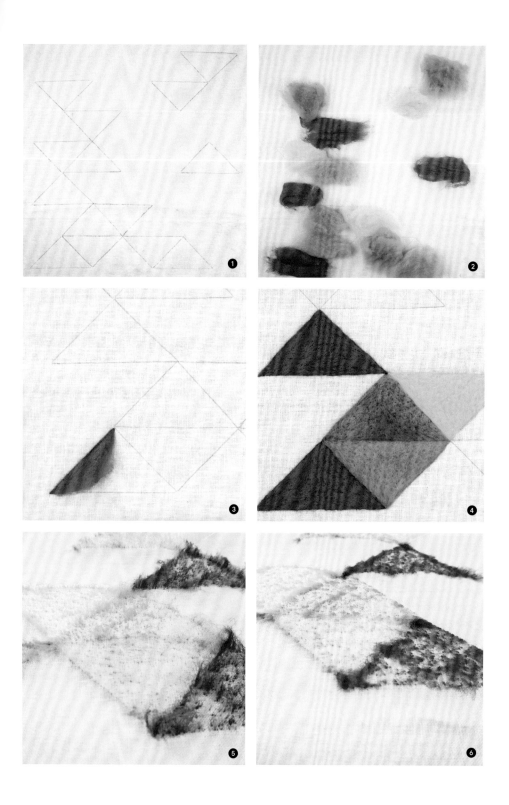

### Prepare the design

Lay out and transfer the triangle pattern to the pillowcase (photo ❶).

Design a color scheme by laying bits of wool over the triangles to determine which color will go where. A quick sketch or photo can help for reference later (photo ❷).

### Felt the triangles

Position the foam pad inside the pillowcase under the design. Your design is likely bigger than the foam pad, so it will be necessary to move the foam pad around after the section on top of the foam is complete. Begin felting the triangles by defining the corners and edges and then filling in the middle (photo ❸). Use the "Poke and Drag" technique (page 30) to get sharp edges.

Felt and fill in as much of the design as fits over the foam pad (photo ❹). Carefully lift the pillowcase from the foam pad and adjust its position over the pattern as necessary.

Continue filling in the shapes and adjusting the position of the foam pad until the design is complete.

### Finish

Insert the pillow form and freshen up your bedroom with this cute, new pillow!

Optional: Turn the pillowcase inside out and iron the fuzzy back-side fibers flat (photos ❺ and ❻). This helps to reduce any raised areas when the pillow form is inserted. Depending on your preference, you can also iron the fibers from the front, which makes the fibers appear more interwoven and a little less bulky. Keep in mind that ironing designs from the front has the potential to change the appearance of the outlines. Any fibers that are not tightly felted into the fabric will likely shift a little. This can be fixed with a couple jabs of a felting needle to reposition the fibers.

Tip. When filling in larger shapes and adding fibers of the same color, overlapping some of the fibers as they are applied next to already felted fibers will help decrease the appearance of any seams. Otherwise, lines or ridges can occur if a new chunk of wool is felted adjacent to another section without any fiber overlap.

# Botanical Curtains

Choosing curtains for a room is difficult for me, so I tend to lean on neutrals. But having the option to personalize them with my own design and color choices allows me to create exactly what I want. This project offers a big impact with a simple design. I chose to personalize a pair of velvet curtains, because the combination of textures is unique. It's such a beautiful contrast of shiny luster versus soft and fibrous. This leaf and its variations lend themselves well to hand-drawing, rather than using a pattern or a stencil. You can even freehand the wool onto the panel, but I recommend drawing lines and making a plan for this project for a couple of reasons. Curtain panels are large, and planning the composition will make finishing the project much easier. Do this by spreading the panel on the floor or a large surface and placing either paper or wool down to represent the future leaves. Move them around until you're satisfied with the placement, then mark where they will go. Another reason to pre-plan is that velvet doesn't like to be overworked with felting needles—the needles can leave noticeable marks. Knowing exactly where the outline is and where the wool should go will minimize any stray needle marks.

**Approximate Time to Complete: 3 to 6+ hours***

*Completion time will vary greatly depending on how large your designs are and how many you add to each panel.

## Supplies

Pen

Velvet curtains (shown in light pink)

Foam pad

Size 38 star felting needle

Carded wool batt (shown in dusty rose)

### Prepare the design

Draw a design onto your curtain panels, then place the curtain panel over a foam pad so the design is centered over the foam pad (photo ❶). If you're transferring the pattern, place the curtain panel over the foam pad first and then transfer (see page 34).

### Felt the main stem

Fill in the main stem first using the thin line technique on (page 28) (photos ❷ and ❸).

### Fill in the leaves

Fill in each leaf. I recommend starting at the outer point of each leaf. Anchor the wool into the point and follow the outline of the curved sides as you work your way down to the base of the leaf (photo ❹). If there is excess wool near the base, hold down the wool already felted with one hand and gently pull away the excess fiber, a small amount at a time, with the other.

Fill in the remaining leaves and repeat until the curtains are finished (photos ❺ and ❻).

### Finish

Hang and adore your beautiful new window treatments!

Tip. To keep the overall motif cohesive, make most of the leaves angle slightly toward the top leaf on their own stem. This gives each stem the same directional growing pattern.

# Herb Pouches

Whether you fill them with homegrown herbs or dried blooms from your local farmers' market, these pouches will add botanical goodness to the space around them. Not only for your sweater storage or lingerie drawer, a pouch or two like this filled with lavender can help safeguard your wool and felt stash from harmful insects like moths. The herb pouch is a no-sew project, meant to be easily created and refillable.

**Approximate Time to Complete: 1 to 2 hours**

## Supplies

2 pieces white sheet felt (approximately double the size of the herb sachet insert)

Herb sachet insert*

Foam pad

Herb patterns (page 131)

Pen

4 colors of carded wool batts (shown here in 2 shades of green, 2 shades of purple)

Size 38 star felting needle

*Create your own by filling reusable tea bags with dried herbs. Add essential oils for more potency.

## Prepare the pouch

Cut two pieces of sheet felt identical in size. The herb sachet should have a little room to breathe and shake inside the pouch, so I recommend making the length and width at least double the size of the sachet insert. My sheet felt measures 5" × 4" (13 × 10 cm).

Center the piece of felt to be the decorated piece over the foam pad, and transfer the pattern (see page 34).

## Fill in the design

Using the thin line technique (page 28), felt the stems of the flowers. Then fill in the leaves with the same green. Extend the green of the stem to form a base leaf for the buds **(photo ❶)**.

Fill in the flower buds with the darker shade of purple. To add depth, create and apply a third layer of buds in the center with the lighter shade of purple **(photo ❷)**. Repeat this for the second flower.

Add a darker shade of green to one side of each stem and to the underside of each leaf for added dimension.

## Make the pouch

To create the pouch, you will felt a border through both sheets in small sections **(photo ❸)**. Leaving gaps in the border allows for airflow and scent to go through the pouch—I felted small lines to mimic oversized stitching, but large dots or any kind of curved or angled lines would work, too **(photo ❹)**. Work your way around the pouch, ensuring the corners are well connected and leaving an opening along one side that is large enough to fit the sachet through.

## Finish

Insert the herb sachet, then seal it in with more felting to complete the border **(photo ❺)**. Turn over the pouch and trim any pieces of fuzzy wool that have poked through. Ironing the edges will flatten the fibers further, but be careful not to iron the sachet, especially if it's a material that might melt.

Place the pouch in a drawer, closet, car, desk, etc.—anywhere you'd like a burst of aroma!

This pouch is designed to be easily opened occasionally to refresh the herb sachet. Gently pull the two layers of sheet felt apart to access the herbs **(photo ❻)**. It can be closed again with more felting.

**Tip.** The wool used for the border will be seen from the back side of the pouch. If you would like to minimize its appearance, choose a color that most closely matches the back piece of felt.

If you prefer the look of a full border, create a full border as a part of the original pattern on the top piece only. Join the two pieces by adding the same border color wool in short sections atop the border, effectively leaving gaps without being noticeable from the front.

Tuck a small bit of the border wool into the pouch so that color is always available for when you need to close the pouch again.

# Sunnies Case

Create this cute pouch for your sunglasses while practicing your freehand felting skills. I'm a child of the eighties and nineties who grew up watching *Rainbow Brite* and *My Little Pony*, so rainbows bring me a lovely feeling of nostalgia. I made this project's rainbow more modern by choosing variations of primary colors (pink instead of red, mango instead of orange or yellow, etc.) and letting the background navy color peek through.

You have a few options for making the pouch: a sewing machine, hand stitching, or fabric glue. Sewing the pouch up with a machine will be the most durable, and it takes just a few quick lines of stitching.

Approximate
Time to
Complete:
1 hour

## Supplies

4" × 15" (10 × 38 cm) piece navy sheet felt

Foam pad

Size 38 star felting needle

5 colors of carded wool batts (shown in pink, mango orange, light green, light blue, light purple)

Sewing machine with all-purpose thread in color to match sheet felt

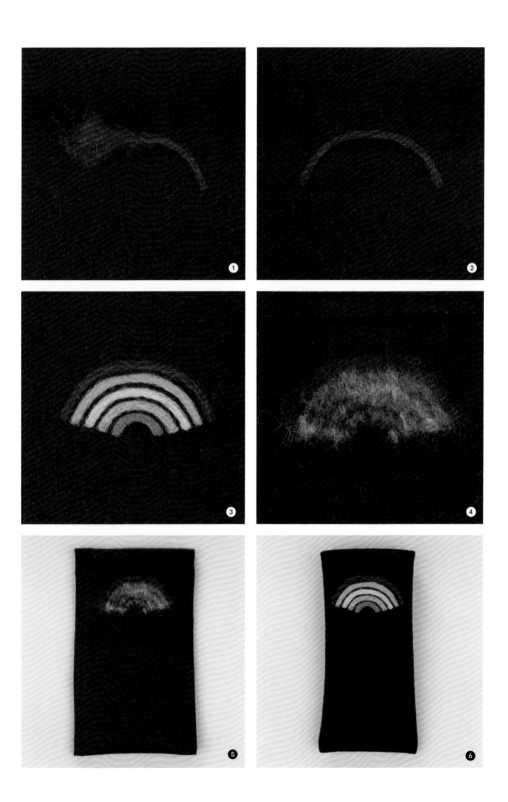

### Create the rainbow

Place the sheet felt over the foam pad and begin felting the top rainbow line, using the thin line technique (page 28) (photo ❶).

Continue adding the rainbow colors, mimicking the curve of the top rainbow line (photo ❷). Leave an even line of empty space between each rainbow color to let the sheet felt peek through (photo ❸).

After all the colors are added, lift the project from the foam pad and iron from the back.

### Sew the pouch

To create a top hem, fold over the felt and sew a hem between ¼ and ½ inch (3–6 mm) wide. Do the same to the opposite end (photo ❹).

Fold the sheet felt in half so that the hemmed edges come together and the pouch is inside out.

Sew each side, leaving a ¼ to ½ inch (3–6 mm) seam allowance, to complete the pouch (photo ❺).

Turn the pouch inside out. Iron the fold if you prefer a crisp bottom edge; iron the felted design if you prefer a more flattened look (photo ❻).

Slide your sunglasses in and marvel at their cute new case!

# 4

# INTERMEDIATE PROJECTS

Layering is a highly useful technique when painting with wool, and the projects in this chapter will help you take this process to a new level. Layers can be bold and thick, or they can be transparent and thin, and you have complete control over how the fibers interact. Use these projects to practice manipulating the wool, making the layers of color bring your pieces to life.

# Peacock Pillow

Approximate Time to Complete: 3 to 3½ hours

## Supplies

Feather pattern (page 132)

Pen

12" × 16" (30.5 × 40.5 cm) natural linen pillowcase

Foam pad

Size 38 star felting needle

12 colors of carded wool batts, shown here as detailed below:

Feather body: dark teal, aqua

Feather quill: white, light gray, dark gray

Feather eye: black, dark gold, dark brown, medium blue, bright green, purple, royal blue

12" × 16" (30.5 × 40.5 cm) pillow insert

This feather is great practice for creating a design by adding each element as a separate layer. Peacock feathers are stunningly beautiful, and their colors can vary depending on the light. I chose to base my feather design in teal and aqua, but feel free to make the main colors of your feather fit your own artistic style or décor.

## Prepare the design

Transfer the feather design to the pillowcase (see page 34). Place the foam pad inside the pillowcase, and center under the design.

## Felt the eye

The feather will be made with a base layer of color followed by a detail layer of highlights and accent colors. Fill in the center of the feather's "eye" using black in the center, then a blue ring, then a dark gold ring. Starting with the eye helps to preserve the shape of the transferred design (**photo ❶**).

## Felt the body

Fill in the body of the feather with a base color—I used deep teal. To create thin lines, follow the steps on page 28. Anchoring the lines on the outer point first will create sharp points for the feather edges (**photo ❷**).

## Felt the stem

Choose a light gray to fill in the shaft of the feather. Pull the fibers to a very thin point, then anchor that point into the eye of the feather. Keep the fibers tight with one hand while gently felting the fibers down the length of the shaft (**photo ❸**). This method will help to keep the fibers going in one direction, creating the illusion of a smooth feather shaft and quill.

## Add detail and dimension

Begin adding more color details. To enhance the blue ring of the eye, add a small amount of green to the top and small amounts of a deeper blue and/or purple to the bottom. Blend the colors into the blue base color by adding thin layers and feathering the edges by brushing them with the tip of the needle. The gold ring is lined on the inner and outer edge with dark brown (**photo ❹**).

To add highlights and texture to the body of the feather, choose a lighter version of the base color. To complement the teal, I chose aqua to make the thin highlight lines (**photo ❺**).

Making sure to outline the feather with these highlights will help it pop against the background fabric.

Lastly, give the feather shaft a bit of detail and depth by adding a darker gray along the edge of the bottom and along one side. Add a highlight by felting in a line of white wool off-center along the opposite side of the shading (**photo ❻**).

## Finish

Clean up any rough edges and make sure the fibers are mostly felted down. Carefully remove from the foam pad. I recommend ironing the design from the back side (after turning the pillowcase inside out), so the design lies flat against the pillow insert.

Add the new pillow to a fancy chair and show off that tail feather!

# Creating Your Own Wool Canvas

**Approximate Time to Complete:**
1 to 1½ hours for an 8" × 10" (20 × 25 cm) piece

**Supplies**

Approximately 1 ounce (28 g) core wool (to create a canvas approximately 8" × 10" × ¼" [20 × 25 × 0.6 cm])*

Foam pad

Size 38 star felting needle

Optional: Multi-needle felting tool or additional 38 star needle to hold two needles at once

*Any wool can be used for this. Core wool is a less expensive and less processed version of carded batts. It is often used in place of dyed wool when larger quantities are required. It's undyed and usually contains a little more vegetable matter than dyed batts.

Oftentimes in two-dimensional needle felting, projects involve felting fibers onto a base fabric, premade garment, or décor piece. But knowing how to create a custom canvas out of wool can be useful for other projects. If an art piece needs a bit of structure or depth, needle felting a base canvas can be the perfect solution. It's also a great choice if the needle-felted fibers need to extend all the way to the edge of a piece. A thicker, handmade wool canvas allows for easier felting along the edges, compared to a flimsier piece of fabric that will likely move as it's poked. The goal for a handmade wool canvas is to create a base that is as dense and as even in thickness as possible. If the wool canvas is too soft or squishy, layering and felting fibers on top will be more difficult, since they are more likely to sink and disappear into the base fibers. Starting off with a "tighter" felting surface is ideal for painting with wool.

Creating a canvas in any size and shape is possible with this technique. Ideally, the foam pad will be larger than the desired canvas size, but it is possible to join pieces together. Just leave the connecting edges unfinished and felt them together using fibers from both sides, adding fibers to mend the seams from the top and bottom.

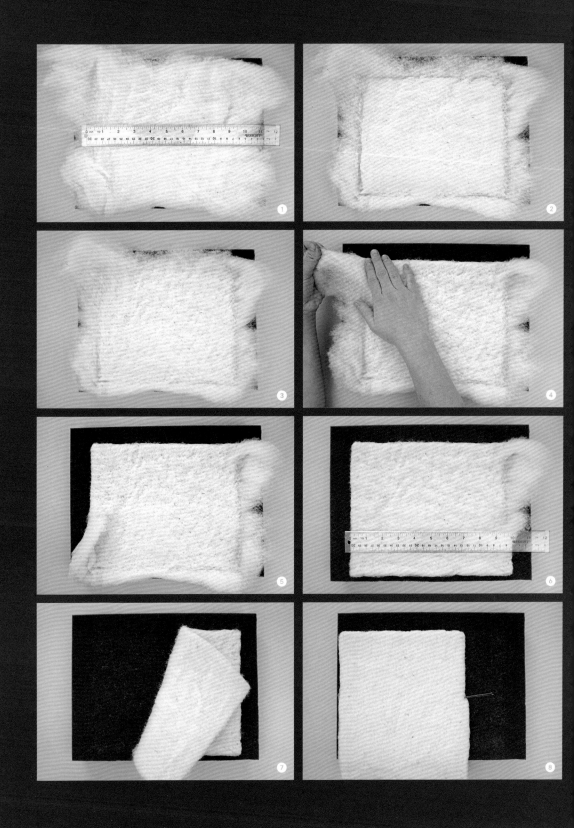

## Measure the wool

Lay out the wool in sheets on the foam pad. It's okay if the foam pad is not as big as your intended final piece; you can simply felt the layers together to achieve your desired dimension. If this is the case, be sure that each piece overlaps the adjacent piece. The sheets of wool should be approximately an inch (2.5 cm) larger on each side than the desired finished size of the canvas. For instance, this project is creating an 8" x 10" (20 × 25 cm) canvas, so the beginning wool sheet is at least 10" x 12" (25 × 30.5 cm) (photo ❶). The wool sheet should be thick enough to block any view of the foam pad. Press down on the wool to determine if any adjustments in thickness can be made now. If there are significantly lumpy areas, either add wool or remove it as necessary. Keep in mind that once the felting process is started, it's much easier to add thickness than to take it away.

## Make the canvas

Create the canvas outline by felting along all sides of the canvas (photo ❷). This will be the actual desired size of the canvas, so measure the length if it needs to be precise. Consider creating this line a bit smaller that the desired finished size, as lifting the canvas from the foam pad may result in some stretching.

Once the edges are defined, begin felting the fibers in the middle. The goal here is to create a bit of density in the middle. This step helps create some structure for the canvas, so it can be lifted and felted from the opposite side (photo ❸). If there are noticeable thin spots, add a bit more fiber. Be careful not to felt too much at this stage, lest too many fibers become anchored in the foam pad. If this happens, more tugging will be required to lift the canvas from the foam, making it impossible not to warp the shape.

Begin creating the final shape of the canvas by folding over the loose wool along the edges toward the middle (photo ❹). While folding and before using the needle, take the time to notice if any section along the edge feels much thicker than the rest. If there are any thick spots, gently remove tufts of fiber a little at a time to even it out.

Continue folding all the edges toward the center (photo ❺). Take care when creating corners, which can become too thick when the fibers from connecting sides overlap.

Once all sides are folded, the canvas should be very close to the final desired size. But it must be condensed more, so carefully lift the entire piece from the foam pad, flip, and felt the entire surface from the other side (photo ❻).

## Finish

Repeat flipping and felting until the canvas is dense (photo ❼). Ideally, when squeezed between two fingers, the canvas will give only a little. When held up to the light, the light should be blocked. (This is also a good technique to discover any thin spots—light will be visible through thin sections. Simply felt on more fibers to thicken where needed.)

If an edge needs to be straightened, use the felting needle at an angle to push fibers inward and/or gently tug on fibers that need to move outward (photo ❽).

# Nighttime in the Forest Wall Art

I love how versatile this project can be. Rather than creating a gradient for the sky, it can be a bold, solid blue. Or, if your sky needs more color, create your perfect twilight by adding in purples, pinks, or oranges with blending and feathering techniques. To create a beautiful gradient sky, choose at least three blues that are of the same hue but different tints and shades. This tutorial shows a blend of five colors that will be applied to create a rounded fish-eye effect to illustrate depth and distance. Create your own intermediary blends by following the process on page 24.

**Approximate Time to Complete: 3 to 4 hours**

## Supplies

7 colors of carded wool batts (shown here in 5 shades of blue for the sky, black, white)

Wool canvas (see page 68) or sheet felt

Foam pad

Size 38 star felting needle

8" × 10" (20 × 25 cm) floating frame

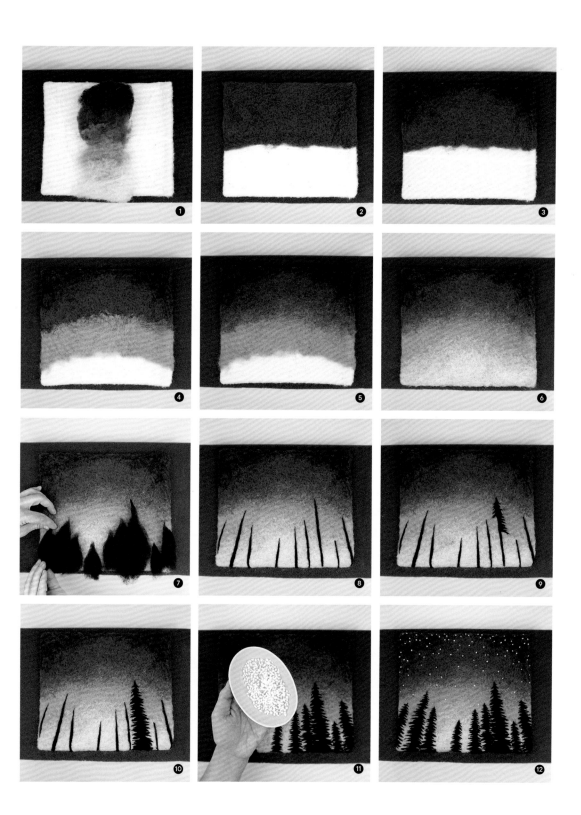

### Create the sky

Working from top to bottom will help to simplify the blending. Choose the color that will cover the most area, and begin to apply that layer to the wool canvas set over a foam pad (photos ❶ and ❷). This color should be one of the darker shades (second darkest) as the sky will brighten toward the horizon.

Using the darkest shade of blue, begin shaping the perspective into the rounded fish-eye effect by adding a thin layer to the corners (photo ❸). Spread the wool out to be transparent and sparse before felting it down. When laid down, the first blue should be visible through the fibers of the darkest blue. To blend the transitions more, use the needle tip to gently brush the darkest fibers toward the center to feather them out, then lightly felt them down.

Add the next band of lighter blue following the rounded shape, blending it into the darker color (photo ❹). A distinct line created during this step will be very hard to blend, so use thin layers and go slowly. If necessary, create an intermediary blend using the two adjacent blues, and begin to layer that on thinly. Feather the fibers so that they are more transparent when laid onto the base (photo ❺).

Continue this process over the whole of the canvas until the sky is finished (photo ❻).

### Add the trees

Placement of the trees can be planned by laying down pieces of wool and rearranging them to create a pleasing composition (photo ❼). If it's helpful, take a photo of the tree placement for reference before starting to felt them on.

Mark the placement of the trees by felting a line for each trunk. The angle of the trunks can help determine branch placement and the direction of growth. To continue the fish-eye effect, the tops of these trees are all slightly pointed toward the middle of the canvas, and the trees in the center are shorter than the trees closer to the canvas sides (photo ❽).

Form the branches of the trees. To get a sharp point at the end of a branch, anchor the wool at the tip of the branch and then work inward to the trunk (photo ❾). Working each individual branch is time-consuming but most effective in creating a realistic silhouette. Alternatively, create two branches at a time with a single line that crosses the trunk. To alter that line a bit, use the needle to push the fibers upward into the trunk to create a slight angle (photo ❿).

### Add stars

Create the tiny stars by rolling a small amount of wool into a ball (slightly damp fingertips can be helpful) and placing it on the canvas in your desired spot (photo ⓫). Secure the star by gently poking along its edges into the canvas (photo ⓬). If poked in the center or too deeply, the ball can disappear below the surface. Add as many stars as you'd like. You can even add your favorite constellations!

### Finish

Frame (or not) and enjoy the view!

# Galaxy
# Place Mats

This project offers a chance to play around with composition in a way that makes nearly any design or pattern look good. By felting a piece of a larger design, it creates a window effect that's like getting a peek of what the larger, implied design might be. Repeating the stripe shape and placement, but changing up the design composition inside the stripe, helps to easily tie multiple pieces together into a coordinating set. It's so easy, it's almost like cheating.

**Approximate Time to Complete: 1 hour or less per place mat**

## Supplies

Ruler

Pen

Set of 4 linen place mats (shown in gray)

Foam pad

12 colors of carded wool batts (shown here in black, dark gray, medium gray, medium blue, dark purple, burgundy, light purple, aqua, peach, bright pink, off-white, white)

Size 38 star felting needle

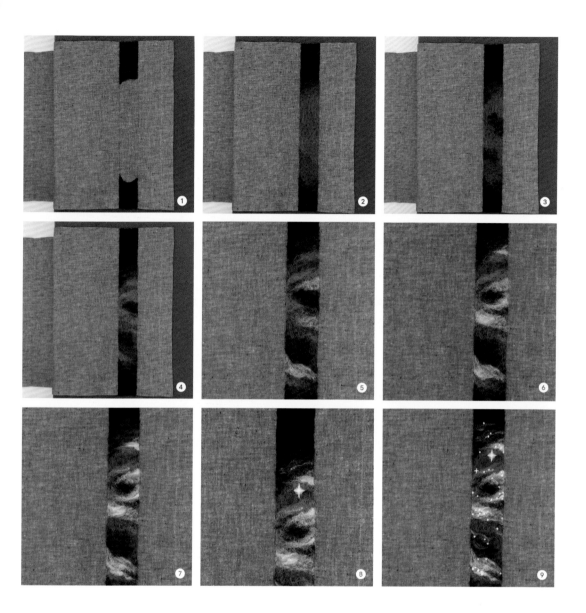

### Prepare the design

Use a straight edge to mark the outlines of the stripe and position the stripe over the foam pad. It's easiest for blending and playing around with the design if the foam pad is large enough to accommodate the entire stripe.

### Felt the sky

Begin placing the base layer of space colors (photo ❶). Most of the bright galaxy colors will be toward the center, so the edges should be darker to imitate the vastness of space. Notice in mine that the black edges blend to gray and then blue in the center (photo ❷).

Next, get creative with colors and layering. For inspiration, study a few galaxy images to plan your color palette. Form the galaxy by laying down small sections of a darker color (photo ❸). Remember, you can always place loose wool on top and play with composition before felting anything down. Working from darker layers to brighter layers will help build visual volume in the galaxy (photo ❹). Keep the layers thin and transparent, allowing colors to peek through from below, like an underpainting.

Keep building the color layers while thinking about general direction, angles, and curvature. Since this stripe is just a "peek" of a larger composition, it's okay to not see where a certain element or color begins. A purple galaxy cloud can sweep across the stripe at one angle and then sweep across again at an opposite angle (photo ❺). This creates movement in the composition and hints that the purple cloud curved at one point outside the "window" of the stripe (photo ❻).

As the color layers get lighter and brighter, use a bit less each time. This intensifies the "light" that is radiating from these galaxy sections (photo ❼).

### Add the stars

To create a super-bright focal star, choose a medium color used in the galaxy cloud and felt a small circle. For the next layer, choose a brighter color (off-white here), and create a curved diamond shape that shows the circle below. Either add a small white circle at its center, or make sure that the diamond color is opaque in the middle for maximum intensity (photo ❽).

Adding stars brings the galaxy to life (photo ❾). Create the tiny stars by rolling a small amount of wool into a ball (slightly damp fingertips can be helpful) and placing it on the canvas in your desired spot. Secure the star by gently poking along its edges. If poked in the center or too deeply, the ball can disappear below the surface.

### Finish

Iron from the back to make sure the place mats lie flat, and have a galactic dinner party!

# Forest Finds Patches

These three patch designs are inspired by my frequent hikes in the woods. I love finding tiny details along the trails and documenting them in my art. Creating a felted patch is a simple project that is easily adaptable in size and color to fit the piece you are attaching it to. Wool sheet felt is a great base for a small patch that will be cut to size, because felt won't fray like other fabrics. Plus, it's thick enough to provide some sturdiness if it's applied to a thinner fabric. Spruce up a denim jacket or small backpack with a forest finds collection of your own!

**Approximate Time to Complete: 1 hour or less per patch**

## Supplies

Small piece of wool sheet felt per patch, color of your choice

Foam pad

Forest Finds patterns (page 133)

Pen

Size 38 star felting needle

Carded wool batts

> Toadstool: 4 shades of red, cream, light brown, white

> Feather: light gray, dark gray, white

> Snail: light brown, dark brown, light green, cream, golden brown

Iron-on adhesive

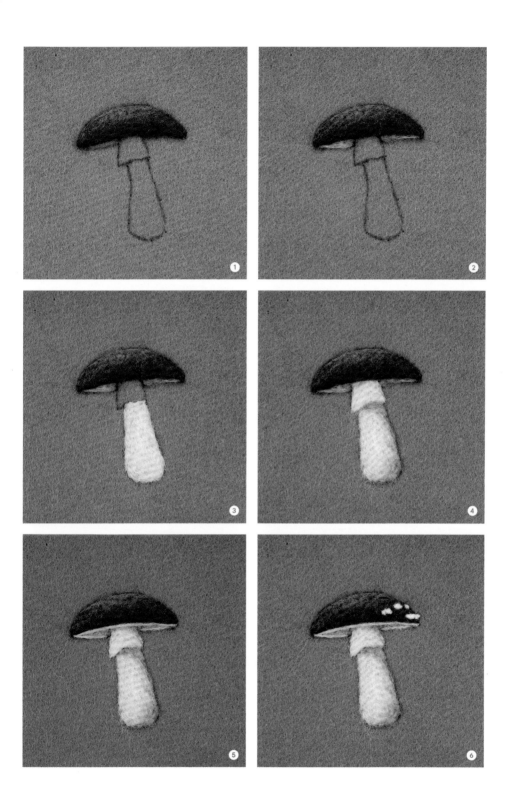

## Toadstool

### Prepare the pattern

Place the sheet felt on the foam pad and transfer the toadstool pattern (see page 34).

### Fill in the toadstool cap

Fill in the toadstool cap with red. Use a gradient of color to add dimension. Add a darker red near the bottom of the cap to indicate a shadow, then apply brighter reds and oranges to the top—the brightest/lightest color should be at the very top (photo ❶).

Fill in the underside of the cap with light brown (photo ❷).

### Fill in the stem

Fill in the bottom half of the toadstool stem with off-white. Add shading on top to the off-white with the same brown used under the cap. The collar of the toadstool (top half of the stem) is shaped like a skirt, so it will cast a shadow on the stem below it (photo ❸).

Fill in the collar of the stem with off-white, and then add the shadow cast by the toadstool cap (photo ❹).

Using the thin line technique (page 28), create an off-white rim along the base of the toadstool (photo ❺).

### Add texture

Create toadstool warts by rolling a small amount of white wool into a ball or oblong shape (slightly damp fingertips can be helpful) and placing it on the canvas. Oblong pieces are great for this project, since they add some imperfection to the toadstool cap (photo ❻).

Secure the wart by gently poking along its edges. If poked in the center or too deeply, the wart can disappear below the surface.

## Feather

### Prepare the pattern

Place the felt on the foam pad and transfer the feather pattern (see page 34) (**photo ❼**).

### Fill in the feather

Fill in the entire pattern with the light gray aside from the center shaft and small wispy feather barbs toward the bottom of the shaft (**photo ❽**).

Add the stripes one at a time, being sure to take the color all the way to the shaft and outer feather edge (**photo ❾**). Keep the stripe borders a little messy for a more natural look (**photo ❿**).

Once the stripes are felted, using the thin line technique (page 28), add the feather shaft.

### Add texture

Give the center shaft shadow and dimension by adding a very thin line of dark gray to one side and along the bottom (end) of the quill.

Add the wispy feather barbs at the base using a very small amount of wool, rolling it into a rope, and anchoring the outer edge first and then connecting it right next to the quill (**photo ⓫**).

Create and add another thin outline along the feather edge to make it stand out against the background felt. I chose white, since it was close in color to the light gray used in the feather but bright enough to be noticed against it (**photo ⓬**).

Snail

## Prepare the pattern

Place the felt on the foam pad and transfer the snail pattern (see page 34) (**photo ⑬**).

## Fill in the snail shell

To keep the spiral line of the shell visible for adding details later, fill in the entire shell with light brown while avoiding felting over the spiral line (**photo ⑭**).

Once the shell is filled in, felt dark brown on top of the spiral line to emphasize it. Using the same dark brown, create a transparent layer that fades into the base color along the parts of the spiral that would be shaded if illuminated from the top. Because this is a small design, just doing the transparent layer on the largest curve on the top and the very bottom of the shell is plenty for added dimension (**photo ⑮**).

To add a little interest in the shell, pick another color that is a similar saturation (easy to blend and not drastically different) to disperse over the top. I added a touch of green to my shell.

Add a highlight on the top of the shell, being sure to follow the curve. Another thin highlight line at the shell opening is a fun detail (**photo ⑯**).

## Fill in the body

Fill in the snail body with golden brown. Give the eyes a bulbous end by adding a small dot of wool and then connecting it to the body with a separate, thin line (**photo ⑰**).

Using the same highlight color from the shell, add a little highlight line along the eyes and down the center of the snail's body. Another thin line under the body of the snail will help it stand out from the background.

Using the same shadow color from the shell, add shading along the edges of the body, eyes, and where the shell and the body meet (**photo ⑱**).

## Finish each patch

After the felted design is finished, trim the sheet felt, leaving a small border around the edge. Trim the fuzzy wool on the back side as close as possible, and then flatten the remaining fuzz with a quick pass of an iron. Follow the instructions of the iron-on adhesive to attach the patch to your jacket, backpack, etc.

# Bunny Brooch

This project steps away from my usual technique of keeping felted pieces as flat as possible by throwing a little relief and volume into the mix. You'll still create depth and dimension with highlight and shadow colors, but dimension will also come from the bulk of the wool added to the surface. It's a fun project that can help you determine if you prefer flatter pieces or the added drama and bulk.

**Approximate Time to Complete: 1 to 2 hours**

## Supplies

2 (3"/7.5 cm square) pieces of sheet felt, in a color similar to the bunny

Foam pad

Bunny pattern (page 134)

Pen

Size 38 star felting needle

6 colors of carded black wool batts (shown here in black, medium brown, dark brown, light taupe, white, peachy pink)

Small, sharp scissors

Fabric glue

Pin back

Hot glue

### Prepare the pattern

Place one piece of felt over the foam pad and transfer the pattern (see page 34) (photo ❶).

### Create the eye

Begin felting the eye with black. Add a bit of volume to the eye, so rather than felting a flat, black circle, make the eye more of a half-dome.

Add a dark brown iris by felting a thin ring inside the black. Leave a black pupil and ring along the outer edge. Notice that I've only added the brown iris for the bottom two-thirds of the eye. This keeps the eye shape and expression more natural, plus the eye-shine spot will cover part of the black space in the next step (photo ❷).

Add a small amount of white wool along the top of the pupil. Be sure to leave an outer black ring (photo ❸).

Add a light taupe ring around the entire eye.

Adjust the black front corner of the eye by extending the line downward (photo ❹).

### Fill in the ears

Fill in the farthest ear with medium brown, being sure to keep the wool bulky. The wool should be firm and not loose and squishy.

Add shadow and highlights to the ear: The darker brown shadows should go around the left edge and base of the ear. Highlight the ear's right side (photo ❺).

Fill in the closer ear with medium-brown wool. Try to keep this wool as bulky as or even more bulky than the farther ear to bring it forward literally and visually.

Fill in the inner ear with peachy pink (photo ❻).

Add a white furry line to the inner ear edge.

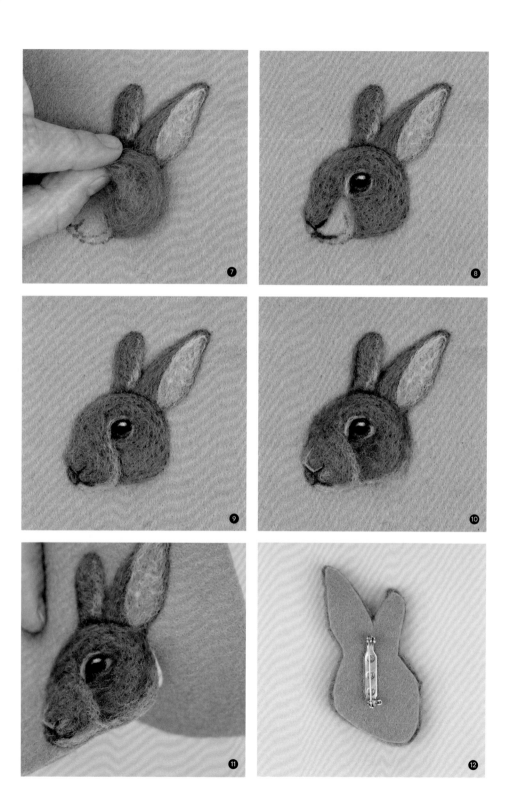

## Add face details

Fill in the bunny's cheek, forehead, and down to the nose. Keep the wool thick right up to the outlines. Exaggerate the separation between the top of the head and ears by poking the needle a few extra times along that line (**photo ❼**).

Using black or dark brown, add the nostrils and the mouth lines (**photo ❽**).

Fill in the rest of the bunny's bulky cheeks. Notice that the cheek line under the eye is still visible.

Using light taupe, add a line under the bunny's chin and cheek and a highlight on the visible cheek line (**photo ❾**).

Add a thin layer of shadows under the eye and along the back and top of the head and forehead. Add a little more shadow color to the left side of each ear.

Redefine the white patches and black line around the eye if necessary and add a touch of highlight to the bunny's cheek just under the nose. Make any last shape or detail adjustments at this point (**photo ❿**).

## Create the brooch

Pull the sheet felt from the foam pad. Using sharp scissors, cut the sheet felt as close to the felted bunny as possible.

Trim the fuzzy wool on the back close to the sheet felt. This is most important along the edges to avoid fuzzy hairs sticking out. Coat the back in fabric glue. Sufficiently coat near the edges, but make sure no excess glue will seep out in the next step (**photo ⓫**).

Place the glued side firmly onto the second piece of sheet felt.

Once dry and secure, trim the second piece of sheet felt, trimming it even smaller than the original so that it's not visible from the front.

Hot-glue the pin back to the back side of the brooch. This brooch is three inches at its longest point from ear tip to nose/mouth, and I used a 1" (2.5 cm) pin back (**photo ⓬**).

Pin the bunny to your lapel and take it on your adventures!

# ADVANCED PROJECTS

These last projects are all about the details. Details are my jam, and I try to pack in as many as I can when I create realistic animals and botanical pieces. The projects in this chapter will help you exercise your artist's eye through the creative use of colors and their values. Think about textures as you work through the steps in this chapter, and how you can portray them with a fiber medium. These projects are a great place to experiment with compositions and test out all your new skills.

# Goldfinch

This male goldfinch is inspired by the many flocks that visit my birdfeeders year-round. I'm an avid birdwatcher, but it wasn't until an ornithology class in college that I realized how remarkable these creatures are. I love to observe birds in my backyard, during forest hikes, and while traveling. The bright, sunny yellow of this goldfinch is sure to be a cheerful embellishment to your wardrobe.

This goldfinch is designed to be perching. Feel free to use a similar pocket position as shown, use another garment feature, or even add a little felted branch for a perch.

My technique with animal wool paintings is to complete the eyes first, and then the nose or beak. This helps to preserve the original shape and allows you to make adjustments to the animal's expression as felting progresses, since sometimes the fibers can shift.

**Approximate Time to Complete: 2 hours**

## Supplies

Foam pad

Chambray button-down shirt*

Goldfinch pattern (page 135)

Pen

2" (5 cm) piece of foam pad**

Size 38 star felting needle

10 colors of carded wool batts (shown here in yellow, cream, white, blue, black, dark mustard, dark brown, pale orange, light peach, light brown)

*I recommend testing a small patch of felting in an inconspicuous spot (that can be pulled out) to make sure the needle and fibers can easily punch through and that the fabric isn't too stretchy.

** The small piece of foam is necessary if you are adding feet to a pocket as shown here. If you're simply felting an entire bird at once, this will not be needed.

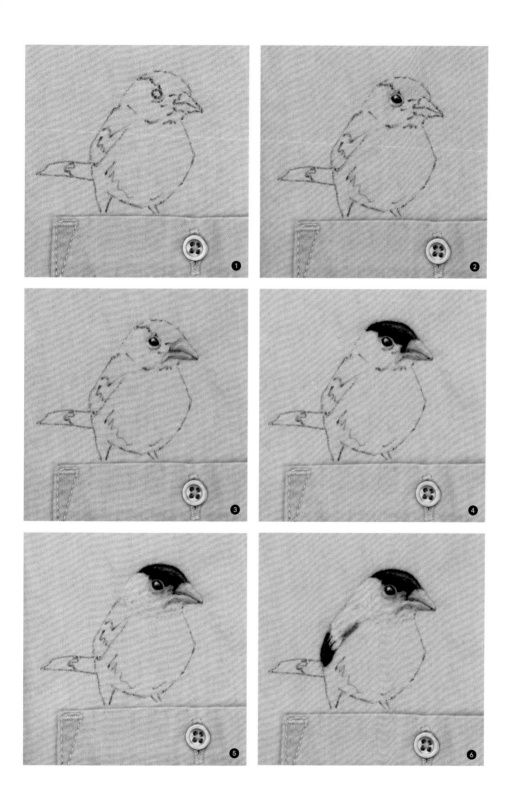

### Transfer the pattern

Place the foam pad under the front shirt layer and transfer the pattern (see page 34) (photo ❶).

### Fill in the eyes and beak

Fill in the eye with black and outline it with the tiniest bit of yellow. This part takes patience and a steady hand. Shallow pokes—only to the first barb—are used for small details like this. To give the eye a sparkle, add white and/or blue wool for the reflection by rubbing a few fibers into a ball and then gently poking along its edges (photo ❷).

To keep the lines of the beak precise, felt the top half before felting the bottom half. For the top half of the beak, felt the main beak color then add a darker shade to mark the beak opening. Add a lighter color on top to highlight and give dimensional shape to the beak.

Repeat these steps (base, shadow, highlight) for the bottom half of the beak (photo ❸).

### Add the head and body color

Fill in the black cap of the goldfinch, being careful to maintain the thin yellow outline around the eye. Add a bit of gray highlight in the direction of its curved head (photo ❹).

Fill in the yellow of the goldfinch's head, making sure the background shirt fabric is covered and the wool is neat (no seams or needle marks), as there won't be much layering here.

Add a bit of shadow with a darker yellow or greenish shade under the bird's eye and where the beak meets the face. Cream or off-white makes a great highlight for yellow, and it can be added along the back of the bird's neck. Extend the highlight of the bird's bottom beak inward toward the cheek to avoid a harsh beak line along the face (photo ❺).

Fill in the yellow, white, and black sections of the bird's wing. An added shadow on the yellow of the wing helps to make it stand out against the bird's body. A gray highlight along the curve of the black wing edge gives it more shape (photo ❻).

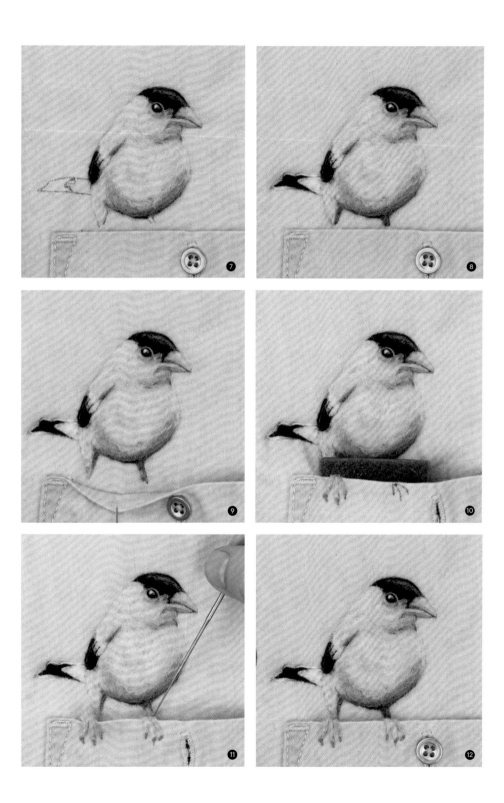

Felt in the remaining yellow of the bird's body and right leg.

Add the yellow shadow color along the lower body's curve. An even darker color can be added as a thin outline along the edge to emphasize dimension. Dark brown is used here (photo **❼**).

Give the right leg a shadow and fill in the left leg with the darker color. Also fill in the black-and-white sections of the tail. Give the black section of the tail a white outline to make it pop against the background (photo **❽**).

Using the same color as the beak, fill in the section of legs not covered in feathers. Consider extending the legs under the pocket flap a bit (if this is your chosen placement) to avoid their looking as if they are cut off from the design (photo **❾**).

## Add the feet

To add the feet to the outer edge of the pocket, a small piece of foam needs to be placed under the pocket edge. Before doing this, very lightly mark with pencil or pen where the tops of the feet visually meet the legs. If not marked, it will be hard to determine correct placement once the foam is under the pocket flap.

Felt the toes with the same color used for the legs. Add a tiny line of highlight to the middle one. Using a very small amount of brown wool, add claws by anchoring in the pointed end first, then securing the other end of the fibers into the toe (photo **❿**).

When releasing the foot fibers from the small foam pad, they may stick up and out the top of the back side of the pocket. Tuck them in by carefully poking the loose fibers downward and into the fibers on the back side of the pocket (photo **⓫**).

## Finish

Carefully lift the design from the foam pad. For wearable felted designs, it's recommended to iron from the back and lightly from the front to maintain flatness. Hand wash only (photo **⓬**).

Enjoy your new bird companion!

# Donut Wall Hanging

One of my favorite guilty pleasures when it comes to creating is food art! And one of my favorite guilty pleasure foods is donuts! It's a win-win. This project is a great way to practice reflective surfaces (the frosting) and shadows and how they are affected by a specific shape. Once you get the hang of creating the highlights and shadows with this version of a donut, get creative and make a series—your own dozen! The wide array of wool colors available really makes the possibilities for donut toppings so fun. Re-create your favorite gourmet treats using this project as a guide for shape and shading. Add sprinkles, frosting stripes, or your favorite flavor of glaze.

Approximate Time to Complete: 2 hours

### Supplies

8"× 9" (20 × 23 cm) piece of white sheet felt

Foam pad

Donut pattern (page 136)

Pen

Size 38 star felting needle

11 colors of carded wool batts (shown here in 4 shades of brown, 4 shades of pink, white, 2 shades of gray)

Magnetic poster frame

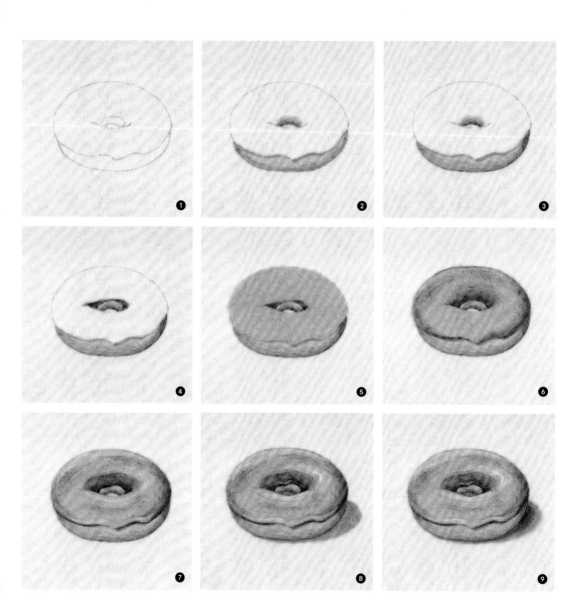

## Transfer the pattern

Place the sheet felt over the foam pad and transfer the pattern (see page 34) (photo ❶).

## Fill in the pastry

Fill in the pastry part of the donut with a light, creamy brown.

Using a darker golden brown, create the shading by adding golden-brown wool underneath where the edge of the frosting will be and along the base of the donut. Don't forget the middle. My imaginary light source is hitting the donut from the top left, causing shadows to be cast underneath and to the right of the frosting layer and the donut as a whole (photo ❷).

Add a little more color (to get that golden, fried look) with a taupe wool next to and mixed into or lightly layered on the golden brown.

Finish the shading with a medium brown. Keep this color to a minimum, but make sure to add it along the edges where you will place the shadow (photo ❸).

## Add the frosting

The pink donut frosting will make use of darker and lighter shades of pink to create dimension. Using a darker (shadow) pink, define the curved line next to the donut's middle. This will be blended in later, but for now you are just marking where it is (photo ❹).

Fill in the rest of the frosting with a light shade of pink (photo ❺).

With the darkest shade of pink, begin to define the edges of the frosting. Concentrate this color along the edges that are dripping over and apply thinner layers along the top part of the donut. Concentrate this pink along the inner edge, too, blending it into the darker shade from the previous step (photo ❻). Apply the darkest shade of pink sparingly along the frosting edges.

With the lightest shade of pink, add highlights by felting thin layers that follow the curve of the top of the donut. Add another thin layer along the dripping frosting edge to give it more volume. Notice the shape of the donut's middle was adjusted a bit with the addition of more medium pink (photo ❼).

For extra shine, add a touch of white wool within the lightest pink sections. A little goes a long way! I added white to the bottom and top part of the inner circle and along the top outer curve of the donut. White was also added to the frosting drips inside the middle of the donut.

## Add a shadow

To add the donut's shadow, keep a few things in mind. Shadows mimic the shape of the object that's casting them, so the donut's shadow will be rounded. Using a medium gray, create a small rounded shadow that follows the bottom part of the donut and extends to the right (photo ❽).

Shadows are often darker the closer they get to the object. Make the shadow darker by adding a hand-mixed combo of the medium gray and the darkest pink used for shading. (See page 24 for more on hand-mixing colors.)

If you want the shadow to fade more into the white background, add the lightest gray along the outer edge of the shadow, feathering it into both the medium gray and the white background (photo ❾).

## Finish

Place your donut in the magnetic frame, hang up your art, and try not to drool.

# Orange & Blossom Table Runner

This table runner project is totally customizable for any piece of furniture. Simply cut a piece of wool felt to the desired length and width. A good rule of thumb is to make the runner about one-third the width of the furniture top and the overhang about six inches on each side, but do what is most pleasing and practical for your home.

Before any felting, cut a simple fringe into both ends. Though wool felt is very durable, keep the fringe wider than ¼" (5 mm) to avoid breakage if pulled (photo ❶).

There are many design possibilities with such a large piece. The sprig of orange and blossoms could be larger and placed so that it creates a ring in the middle of the runner. For high impact and lots of color, the runner can have borders of oranges, greenery, and blossoms. The given pattern can be altered, and different versions of the original (orange with leaves, orange with blossom, blossom only, orange only, etc.) can create the borders.

If preferred, create a few visual options to decide on your favorite composition. Sketch out a few versions on paper or print and cut out multiple patterns to lay down, cut up, and rearrange. My version of the table runner has a border of the original pattern plus variations. This tutorial will be a step-by-step guide to the original pattern, so then each element can be created as a stand-alone later.

**Approximate Time to Complete:** 2 to 3 hours per orange sprig

## Supplies

Foam pad

12" × 36" (30.5 × 91 cm) piece gray sheet felt

Orange & blossom pattern (page 137)

Pen

Size 38 star felting needle

13 colors of carded wool batts, shown here as detailed below:

Orange (7 gradient shades from pale peach to rust orange)

Leaves (light green, medium green, dark blue-green)

Blossom (white, light brown, yellow, orange)

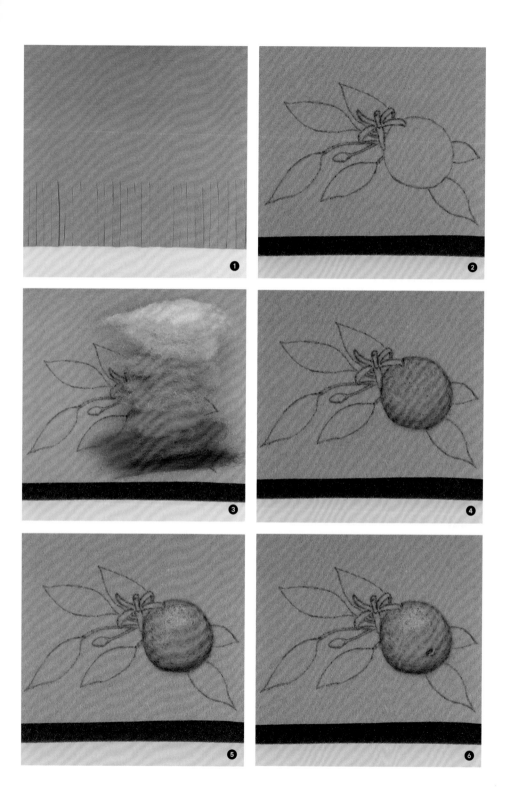

## Prepare the design

Place the foam pad beneath the felt and transfer the pattern onto the felt (see page 34), and gather your color palette (photo ❷). I used three shades of green (base, highlight, shadow), seven shades of orange (more highlights and shadow colors for a three-dimensional effect), and white, light brown, yellow, and orange for the flower elements. Seven shades of orange are certainly not necessary to create a beautiful three-dimensional effect; it can be done using only three colors and creating intermediate shades (see page 24). But other hues can really round out the image: yellow can be used as a highlight; brown or muted reds like burgundy could be used as a shadow (photo ❸).

## Add color and dimension to the fruit

Fill the orange in with the medium shade. To illustrate dimension, decide on an imaginary light source and the direction from which it's shining. Here, the light source is coming from the top. Apply a shadow color (a darker shade of orange) along the side opposite the light source. Be sure to follow the curve and shape of the orange (photo ❹).

If an even deeper shade is available, following the same curve, add a small amount to the very edge of the orange. Often the deepest shades of a shadow are the smallest in area for an object that is softly lit.

Next, add a highlight color. Continuing with the curve created for the shadow, apply the highlight wool in a rounded shape on the side of the orange closest to the light source. If available, add more highlighting colors in smaller amounts concentrically to finish the 3D illusion (photo ❺).

To add a navel, connect two semicircles using one shadow and one highlight color. Use the shadow color for the semicircle closest to the light source and the highlight color for the semicircle farthest from the light source. Using the inverse of the highlight and shadow colors of the orange, a recessed illusion is accomplished (photo ❻).

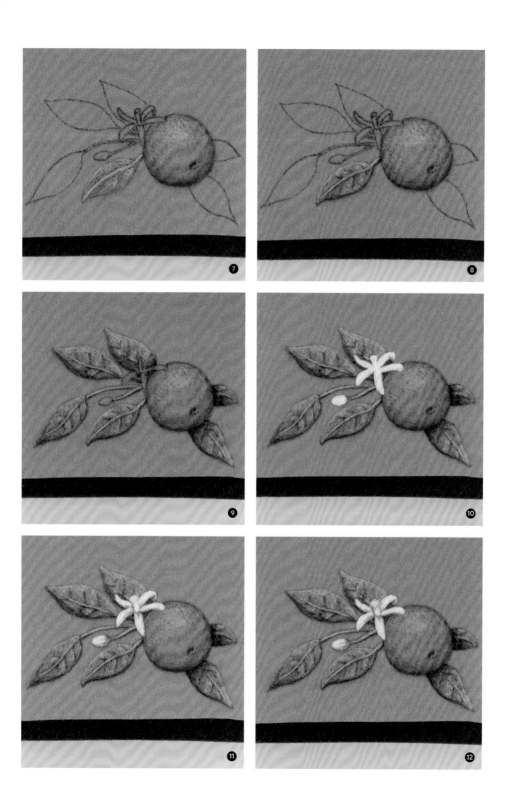

## Give the leaves color and detail

The leaves are done in a similar layering fashion, while keeping in mind the same directional light source used for the orange. Fill in with the base color (medium) green.

Using the highlight color, add a center vein extending from the stem, but stop short of the point of the leaf. Giving the center vein a bit of a curve will show dimension and give a little movement. A middle vein added a little to one side can give the impression that the leaf is naturally rotated (photo **7**).

Add a few more highlights as if the light source is hitting the body of the leaf. This leaf would be illuminated mostly along the top edge, but also some light would be hitting the curvature of the leaf on the other side, especially if the leaf is rotated slightly upward.

With the shadow color, add the shading on the opposite parts of the leaf. Using the same color, create depressions in the leaf by felting lines where veins would be extending from the center vein—notice in the leaf body that the shadow color is applied directly next to the highlight color on the side closer to the light source to achieve this (photo **8**).

Continue the same process (base, highlight, shadow) on the remaining leaves and flower stems. Be sure to work around the flower shapes if you need those for guidance later (photo **9**).

## Fill in the flowers

Fill in the flower and bud with white (photo **10**).

Create the separate petals and shading on the bud with a very small amount of light brown.

Top the center of the flower with yellow wool to represent the pistil (photo **11**).

Create small orange balls to add around the pistil to represent the stamen (photo **12**). Gently poke each ball along its edge to secure in place. Be careful not to poke too deeply or in the center, as it could disappear below the felt.

## Finish

Iron the back side of your table runner, then spruce up your next table setting with this burst of citrus.

# Floral Cardigan

I love flowers in all settings—freshly picked in a vase, painted and framed, or a pattern dyed on my favorite dress. So creating a cheerful floral sweater was first on my list of projects for this book. In fact, most pieces in your wardrobe can be personalized with your favorite needle felted florals. Any piece of clothing with a felted design will need to be hand-washed to minimally disturb the fibers. Needle felted embellishments on clothing are not necessarily permanent and should be cared for sensibly. The level of detail in the final design needs to be considered when adding to clothing. You may need to touch up the felting or repair a snagged fiber at some point, and the less fine detail there is, the easier the repairs will be.

I added a bouquet of multicolored pansies to this creamy wool sweater for a pop of brightness. Pansies are a great choice for keeping the same general flower shape but completely changing the individual bloom colors. Research different colors of pansies to pick your favorites.

I played around with multiple copies of the single pansy and leaf patterns, cutting them and placing them on the sweater to come up with the final composition. Two pansy views are provided so you can determine what works best for your piece. Feel free to cut/tape/trace your way to your own version. I was sure to try on the sweater and mark the area that I wanted to felt with a couple of straight pins. This way my design is completely customized to my sweater and body. Because— let's be honest—nothing ruins an otherwise great top more than a poorly placed pattern!

**Approximate Time to Complete: 6 to 8 hours**

## Supplies

Wool cardigan*

Foam pad

Flower pattern (page 138)

Pen

Size 38 star felting needle

10+ colors of carded wool batts (shown here in shades of pinks, purples, white, yellow, peach, light green, medium green, blue green)

*Many different fiber blends are potentially good bases for felting, but wool naturally accepts the additional wool fibers. For other textiles or articles of clothing, the fabric shouldn't be too stretchy or bulky. Test other fabrics in an inconspicuous place to ensure they will work.

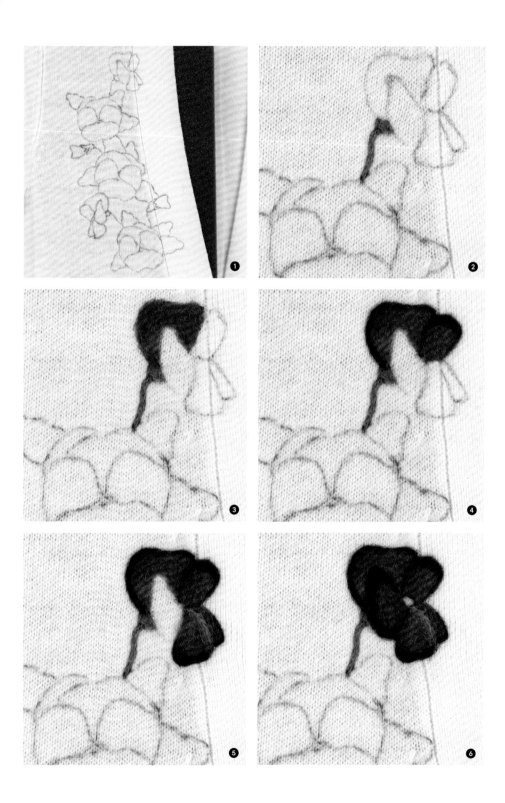

### Prepare the design

Place one side of the sweater over the foam pad and transfer the pattern (see page 34). I decided to work from top to bottom on this piece to minimally disturb the design as it's felted. Notice that the order of felting is from background to foreground, including the individual petals of each flower. When done this way, the fibers of the foreground piece can literally sit on top of the background piece, helping to more easily create visual depth and keep any line corrections to a minimum (**photo ❶**).

### Flower 1

Fill in the green stem and flower base (**photo ❷**).

Each petal is the same color: fuchsia with a darker burgundy edge (**photo ❸**). Fill in each petal in the order of farthest to nearest (**photo ❹**).

Add a small highlight to the lower petal to create the natural fold (**photo ❺**).

Once all petals are felted, add a small white center (**photo ❻**). Roll the wool between your fingers to make a small, loose ball. Apply it by gently poking along its edges.

**Tip.** When felting on an article to be worn, be sure to felt the entire surface of the design as best as you can. For example, you can fill in a leaf by felting along the edges and flattening the wool in the middle with just a few pokes. Even though that wool in the middle is flush to the sweater with just a few pokes, go over the area a little extra to help anchor the fibers into the sweater and prevent fiber movement with wear.

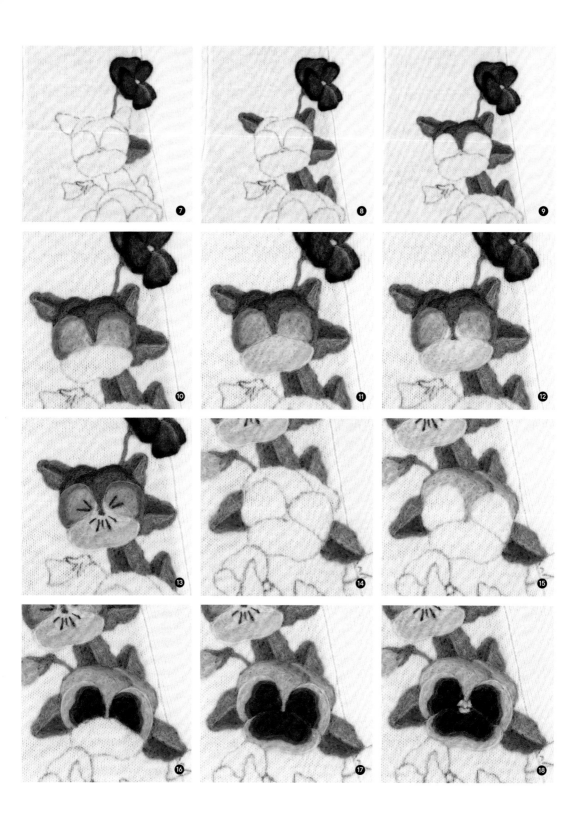

## Flower 2

Fill in all the green leaves that are behind this pansy with a medium green. Then add a light layer of blue-green to half of each of these leaves (photo **7**).

Add a light layer of light green to highlight the other half of each leaf. Rather than focusing on a directional light source for these leaves, I chose the shadow and highlight halves by what looked best according to the nearest flower (photo **8**).

The petals on this pansy are darker in the background and get lighter as they come forward. Fill in the two petals in the back with a rich blue-purple and give the edges a darker purple border (photo **9**).

The two symmetrical middle petals are a light purple with a medium purple border (photo **10**). The largest petal on the bottom is an even lighter purple with a white border (photo **11**).

Add a light layer of yellow to the center of the bottom petal and a touch of white to the center of the middle petals (photo **12**).

Finally, add dark purple lines (page 28) to the middle and bottom petals (photo **13**).

## Flower 3

I decided to make the pansy buds the same color as the flower from which their stem is sprouting. This pair will have light pink outer petals with a touch of yellow, so the bud is simply that.

Before filling in the pink petals of the open pansy, felt the green stem and leaves sitting behind it the same way you did the leaves for the previous flower, deciding which side of each leaf is the shadow and which is the highlight as you please (photo **14**).

The back two petals are light pink with a touch of peach toward the center and darker pink along the edges (photo **15**).

The middle petals have light pink edges with a touch of yellow, a dark burgundy center, and a fuchsia line bordering the two. Add an off-white edge to the light pink part of the petals to separate it from the petals behind them (photo **16**).

The bottom petal is the same as the middle two. Repeat the off-white edge here, too (photo **17**).

Finally, add small amounts of white to the very base of the three foreground petals and a little bit of yellow in the very center the way you added the white at the center of the first flower (photo **18**).

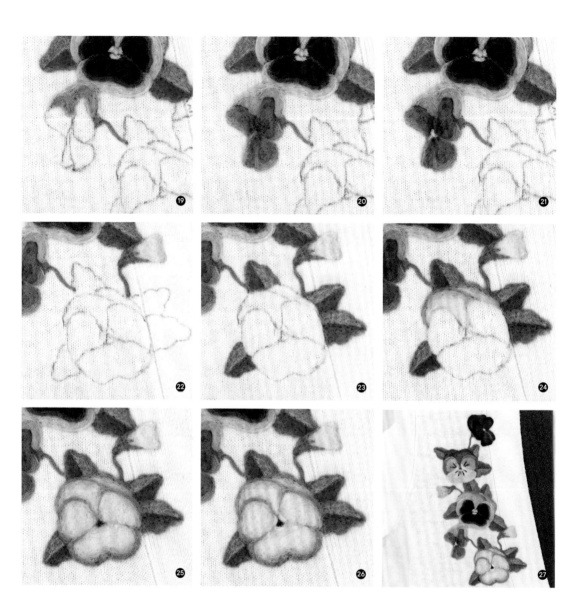

## Flower 4

Felt the green stem and flower base.

Like Flower 1, work background to foreground to felt the petals. The farthest petal is a light purple, with an even lighter purple edge (**photo ⑲**).

The remaining petals are a medium purple that fades to a deeper purple toward the center of the flower (**photo ⑳**).

Add a thin, dark purple edge to the middle petals for definition (see page 28).

Add some yellow to the center of the pansy (**photo ㉑**).

## Flower 5

This bud and open flower pair will be yellow with a touch of pink. Fill in the bud with yellow and add a light layer of pink toward the edge (**photo ㉒**).

Fill in the green stem and base and all the remaining leaves (**photo ㉓**).

The background petals for the open bloom are yellow with light pink and darker pink along the edges (**photo ㉔**).

Repeat the same pattern for the middle petals, adding a light layer of a bolder yellow near the flower center.

The bottom petal follows the same pattern as the previous two with a small center of dark burgundy (**photo ㉕**). Finish the flower center with a small amount of white on each of the three petals near the flower center (**photo ㉖**).

After the design is finished, make sure there aren't spots of looser fibers. Anchor them into the sweater with a few extra pokes of a needle if necessary (**photo ㉗**).

Repeat the steps for the other side. You can create an exact mirror of the first design or change up the composition or color.

## Finish

Iron the felted design on both sides to flatten any bulkiness. Pair with a cute dress or skinny jeans and amazing shoes!

# Panda Portrait

My body of work is mostly portraits or portrayals of animals, and this is not by accident. I grew up wanting to work with them and ended up doing so as a conservation educator in my first career. My job was to teach people about animals and habitats so that they could make a connection and feel inspired to effect change. My goal as an artist is the same: to foster the connection that humans have with animals. I chose this panda portrait because giant pandas are the quintessential representation of endangered animals in our time. They are struggling to survive in a world of human encroachment and deforestation causing lack of food and habitat. But they are adored and the target of conservation efforts worldwide.

We can make a difference on this planet, and we should certainly try. For now, as you practice and complete this panda portrait, spend a moment thinking about what changes you'd like to see in the world and the steps you could take to effect that change. Let your finished panda portrait be a reminder of those aspirations—and then MAKE THE CHANGE.

**Approximate Time to Complete: 3 to 4 hours**

## Supplies

10" (25 cm) diameter piece natural tan linen

Foam pad

Panda pattern (page 139)

Pen

Size 38 star felting needle

8 colors of carded wool batts (shown here in white, black, brown, blue, peach, light gray, medium gray, dark gray)

8" (20 cm) diameter embroidery hoop

Scissors

Acid-free cardstock, cut to fit inside the back of the embroidery hoop (optional)

Hot glue

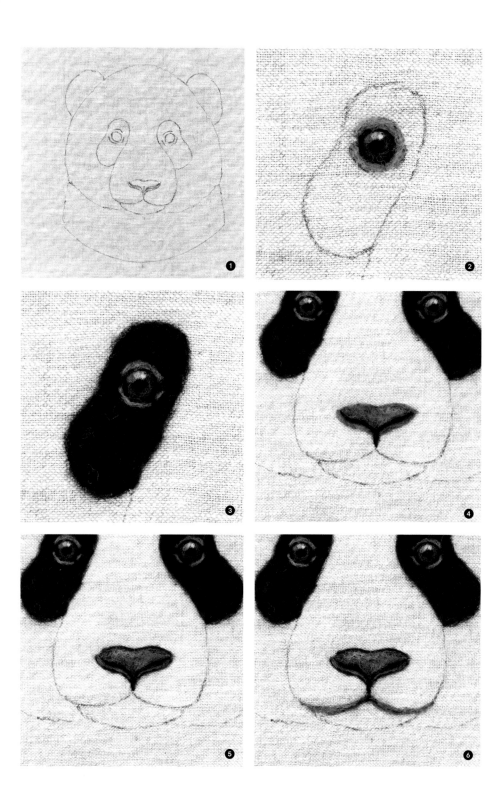

### Prepare the pattern

Place the linen on the foam pad and transfer the pattern (photo ❶).

### Fill in the eyes

As I mentioned in the goldfinch design (page 97), I always complete the eyes first. Fill in an entire eye with black. Layer on a brown iris in a circle, leaving a black pupil and black edges around the eye (photo ❷).

Add sparkle to the eye with a few color highlights. I love adding blue, peach, and white for dramatic eyeshine. Add these in small amounts, following the eye's natural curve.

Give the eye a border of medium-gray eyelids.

Fill in the eye patch with solid black (photo ❸).

Repeat for the other eye.

### Fill in the nose

Fill in the nostrils with black. I like to define the nostrils first so as not to lose their shape while filling in the rest of the nose. The lines can be redefined later if necessary.

Using dark gray, fill in the remaining empty parts of the nose (photo ❹).

Define the nose edges with a small line of black, using the thin line technique on page 28.

Add a highlight to the nose with the same colors used for the eye sparkle. Thin, transparent layers will be less dramatic and suggest a softer texture than solid spots of highlights (photo ❺).

### Fill in the mouth

Cover the mouth lines with a mixture of dark gray and black. Concentrate a little more black below the nose and in the center of the mouth (photo ❻).

### Fill in the ears

Fill in the ear fur with black and add texture and tufts by bringing the wool to a point along the ear edges. Guide the direction of the tufts by following the curve of the ear, rather than making them stick straight out like they're radiating from the center of the face. Add a few lines of dark gray on top of the black to create more dimension (photo ❼). As with the tufts, follow the curve of the ear. Lastly, use a bit of medium gray along the outer edges of the black ear fur for added dimension (photo ❽).

Repeat for the other ear.

### Fill in the body

Fill in the body of the panda with solid black. Add texture lines in dark and medium gray in the direction that the panda's fur would naturally grow. A little goes a long way in this step. Like the ears, line the outer edge of the black body with medium gray for dimension. The illusion here is that the gray is portraying light reflected on the tips of the black fur along the sides of the panda's body (photo ❾).

### Fill in the face

Solidly fill one side of the panda's face with light gray. Leave the snout untouched for now. Since it's in the foreground, that will be last to complete. Take a bit of the light gray into the black eye patch with small lines. This suggests the texture of fur (photo ❿).

Add a little bit of shading as shown with a medium gray and a medium/light gray mixture. Start creating a bit of textural movement with these shading grays by felting directional lines. The fur on this part of the panda's face will be growing outward and downward (photo ⓫).

Using the same directional felting, begin adding a white top layer. Concentrate the white along the edge of the panda's face. Make it thicker by adding bold V shapes (photo ⓬).

Add white directional fur along the black eye patch, too.

Repeat for the other side of the panda's face.

## Complete and refine

Fill in the panda's forehead by adding a layer of light gray and topping it with directional white wool. Concentrate white along the top of the panda's head. The fur along the panda's forehead and between the eyes will have a natural vertical direction (photo ⓭).

Fill in the chin with light gray and add tufts along the bottom edge.

Use medium gray to add a bit of shading along the chin curvature.

Add small lines of white on top to highlight the fur texture (photo ⓮).

Fill in the remaining part of the snout with light gray.

Add medium-gray shading to the bridge of the nose between the eyes and to the areas underneath and above the nose. Use a light touch with this shading and keep it smoother than the cheek sections. The fur on the panda here will be shorter and less textural. Bring the nose farther into the foreground by adding white to the edges, from the upper part of the eye patches to the center of the mouth (photo ⓯).

Redefine the edges of the nose by adding more black wool.

Soften the snout edges by adding a little white texture under the eye patches on each side. This will help to blend the thicker white of the snout into the gray of the cheeks.

Add a little texture into the black eye patches by adding a very small amount of dark gray fibers in the shape of a smile under the eyes (photo ⓰).

Lastly, make the panda visually pop against the background (if it's a light color, like mine) by giving the white fur a thin border of medium gray. Tuck this border under the white by using the needle at a 45-degree angle or less (photo ⓱).

## Finish

Remove from the foam pad, and iron if desired (photo ⓲). To permanently frame it in the embroidery hoop, separate the inner and outer parts of the embroidery hoop. Center the panda design over the smaller, inner hoop.

Loosen the fastener until the outer hoop slides easily over the linen and onto the inner hoop. Centering a design in an embroidery hoop can take a little trial and error. If the design is initially off center, remove the outer hoop and reposition the fabric (photo ⓳).

Once the work is in place, tug the edges of the linen so that the panda design is flush with the hoop at the bottom and there are no wrinkles or puckers.

Once straightened and taut, tighten the fastening screw.

Trim the edges of the fabric so that when folded over the back side of the inner hoop, just enough remains to glue to the inside. Keep in mind that too much fabric can push on the back side of your art and look bumpy when folded over. Optional: You can protect the back side of the piece (from dust or excess touching) by adding a circle of acid-free cardstock or even wool felt before you fold over and glue the edges.

Using hot glue or fabric glue, add small lines of glue at a time onto the wooden hoop and then fold the fabric over. Hold until secure (photo ⓴).

Hang your hoop on the wall by setting the fastener on a nail or hook, display on a shelf, or add ribbon or twine and hang with fancy washi tape (photo ㉑).

# PATTERNS

# Moon Phase Tote Bag

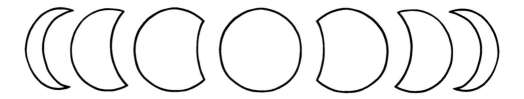

# Herb Pouches

rosemary

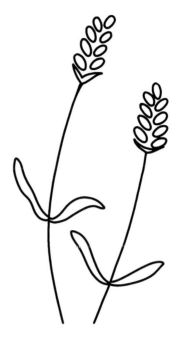

lavender

eucalyptus

# Forest Finds Patches

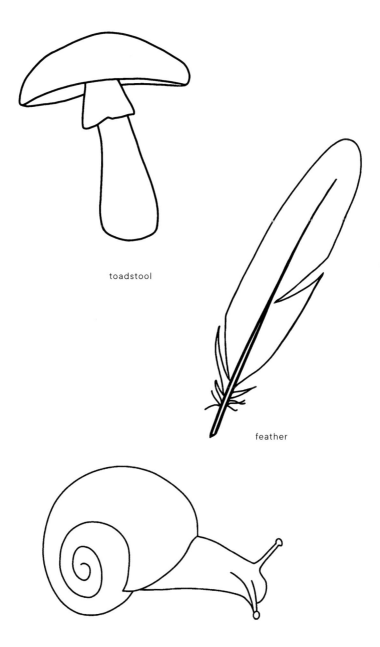

toadstool

feather

snail

## Bunny Brooch

# Goldfinch

# Panda Portrait

# ACKNOWLEDGMENTS

I owe heaps of thanks to the people who helped make this book possible. Firstly, I'd like to say a special thank-you to all my students, past, present, and future. Your eager willingness to learn new skills and invest in your creativity will always be an inspiration to me and help me strive to push the boundaries of my art.

To my editor, Meredith Clark, and to my entire team at Abrams, thank you for helping me share my vision and bring the best version of this book into the world. A huge thanks to my agent, Lindsay Edgecombe, for always being my advocate. Furthermore, I'm particularly grateful to Janae Hardy and Rachel Denbow, for making all my photo dreams come true. You two have skills that are unmatched.

To my family and friends, thank you for your constant encouragement and support. To my mom especially, thanks for always being my biggest cheerleader and for keeping me level-headed. A very special thank-you to Teresa Drummond, for kicking off my new life trajectory when you introduced me to needle felting. I will forever be grateful for our friendship. And finally, to my husband, Brandon, thank you for being whatever I needed at just the right time. I couldn't have done this without you.

# RESOURCES

Here are some great shops that I find myself frequenting for projects.
You can also take a look at my website to find even more and updated
information about these resources and beyond.

Living Felt Felting Supplies
www.livingfelt.com

DyeingHouseGallery/DHGshop
www.dhgshop.it

Weir Crafts
www.weircrafts.com

The Woolery
www.woolery.com

Peace Fleece
www.peacefleece.com/shop/

Sarafina Fiber Art, Inc.
www.sarafinafiberart.com

World of Wool
www.worldofwool.co.uk/

Etsy
www.etsy.com

Big Sky Fiber Arts
www.bigskyfiberarts.com

Favorite pens, available where crafting supplies are sold:
Uni-ball Signo Gel Grip, Fine Tip Sharpie

Editor: Meredith A. Clark
Designer: Heesang Lee
Production Manager: Michael Kaserkie

Library of Congress Control Number: 2018936259

ISBN: 978-1-4197-3444-1
eISBN: 978-1-68335-515-1

Copyright © 2019 Danielle Ives
Photography by Janae Hardy

Cover © 2019 Abrams

Printed and bound in China
10 9 8 7 6 5 4 3 2 1

Abrams books are available at special discounts when purchased in
quantity for premiums and promotions as well as fundraising or educational
use. Special editions can also be created to specification. For details,
contact specialsales@abramsbooks.com or the address below.

**ABRAMS** The Art of Books
195 Broadway, New York, NY 10007
abramsbooks.com